THE PILMOOR BOROUGHBRIDGE AND KNARESBOROUGH RAILWAY

Patrick Howat

Published by Martin Bairstow, Fountain Chambers, Halifax, West Yorkshire
Printed by Allanwood Press Ltd, Pudsey, Leeds

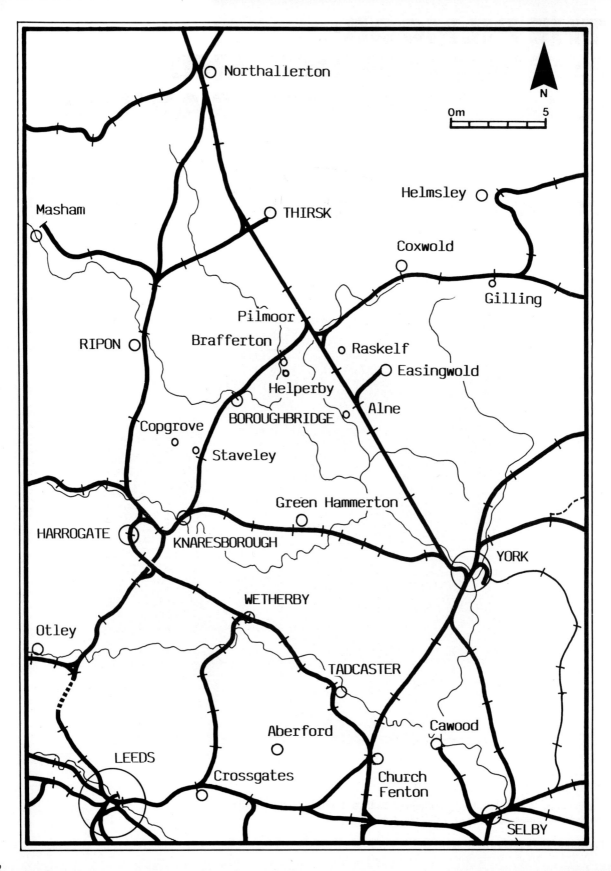

Northallerton

N

0m   5

Masham

THIRSK

Helmsley

Coxwold

Gilling

Pilmoor

Brafferton

RIPON

Raskelf

Easingwold

Helperby

BOROUGHBRIDGE

Alne

Copgrove

Staveley

Green Hammerton

HARROGATE

KNARESBOROUGH

YORK

WETHERBY

Otley

TADCASTER

Cawood

Aberford

LEEDS

Crossgates

Church
Fenton

SELBY

1 History

1835–1845

The first railways of the north of England connected the hinterland with the North Sea ports, principally for goods traffic. In the early 1830s railways began to be built to connect important towns together for both passengers and goods. In 1835 the North Midland Railway was proposed, from Derby, where it connected with the Midland Counties Railway, to Leeds. In the same year the York and North Midland Railway (Y&NM) was formed to bring a line from Altofts, on the North Midland Railway, to York. By these means both Leeds and York were provided with a link to the south and to London.

It was also in 1835 that the matter of the northwards extension from Leeds and York began to exercise the minds of the entrepreneurs of both cities. But it was Joseph Pease of Darlington who took the first step, by proposing the Great North of England Railway (GNE). Not surprisingly the businessmen of Leeds wanted the line to the north to emanate from that city rather than from York. The GNE therefore proposed two lines, from Leeds and from York respectively.

All railway proposals from Leeds to the north had to contend with the fact that Leeds is in the valley of the River Aire, unlike York which lies in a broad plain. A railway north from Leeds had either to cross from one river valley into another – from the Aire to the Wharfe, to the Nidd, to the Ure, to the Swale – or to avoid the valleys altogether by going eastwards towards the Plain of York. The GNE line from Leeds chose the latter option by going via Aberford, Wetherby, Knaresborough and Boroughbridge. (The later Leeds and Thirsk Railway chose the former option.) From York the GNE ran northwards via Easingwold. The two lines converged near Ripon and ran to the River Tees.

The promoters of the GNE realised that the northern part of their line, from the River Tees to Newcastle, would take longer to construct than the southern part. They reasoned that by commencing the northern part a year earlier the whole line would be ready simultaneously. Acts of Parliament for the northern section of the GNE, the North Midland Railway and the Y&NM, were passed in 1836.

The southern section of the GNE received its Act in 1837 but it omitted the branch from Leeds. Moreover, in the words of W.W. Tomlinson in his *The North Eastern Railway, Its Rise and Development*, the GNE considered that 'a grand national railway ought not to be materially diverted from a direct course to serve merely local or partial interests'. The GNE therefore ran its line from York to the River Tees in as straight a line as it was possible to find. It even, in an act of considerable prescience, contemplated purchasing land for a quadruple line, for when 'the time might come when goods might be carried at the rate of 30 miles an hour, and when passengers would not be content with travelling less than 60'.

By 1840 the Y&NM and the North Midland Railway were open. The southern section of the GNE from York to Darlington was opened to goods on January 1st 1841 and to passengers on March 30th the same year. The northern section, on which no work had been done, was later adopted by the Newcastle and Darlington Junction Railway (N&DJ), using a route different from that intended by the GNE.

For the time being, however, the only outlet from Leeds to the north remained via York and the GNE, a situation that did not please the commercial interests of Leeds. In 1844 the GNE published plans for a new line from Pilmoor, north of York, to Harrogate via Boroughbridge and Knaresborough, with a branch from Boroughbridge to Ripon. The Leeds businessmen responded with their own new line to the north via Starbeck (near Harrogate) and Ripon. The Leeds and Thirsk Railway (L&T) was born. The Y&NM for its part proposed a line from Church Fenton to Harrogate, to give the latter town an outlet to the south in preference to the L&T.

Discussions took place between the GNE and the L&T, the GNE hoping that the L&T would confine itself to a line from Leeds to Harrogate connecting with its branch from Pilmoor. Neither company was willing to compromise so the GNE proposed extending its Pilmoor to Harrogate line to Leeds via Spofforth and Rigton, in direct competition with the L&T. The L&T and GNE went to Parliament with their Bills.

At this stage George Hudson's influence was growing. By 1845 he controlled the Y&NM and the N&DJ. In May that year he took a lease of the GNE and at once ordered abandonment of the proposed branches from Pilmoor to Harrogate and Leeds and from Boroughbridge to Ripon. This left the way clear for the L&T which obtained its Act in 1845 and was opened in 1849. The Act for the Y&NM branch from Church Fenton to Harrogate was obtained in 1845 and the line was opened in 1848 and 1849.

Although the GNE's branch from Pilmoor to Harrogate and Leeds was abandoned on the orders of George Hudson, the Company did not altogether lose interest in the area through which it was to have passed.

In its strategy of not materially diverting from a direct course to serve merely local or partial interests the GNE's route from York to Darlington was admirably direct, a feature that has been invaluable in the quest for higher speeds. But in deliberately avoiding most intermediate towns, the Company deprived itself of potentially lucrative traffic. Only Thirsk and Northallerton were on the railway and even Thirsk station was more than a mile from the town centre. Other towns such as Easingwold and Boroughbridge lay several miles from the line.

In 1846 the GNE obtained Acts for the construction of three branches, one of which was from Pilmoor to Boroughbridge. Shortly after this the GNE was absorbed into the N&DJ which became the York and Newcastle Railway.

Why did the GNE choose this particular branch? Was it merely to connect Boroughbridge, a market town of some importance and on several stage coach routes, with its main line? That is the simple explanation but there may be more to it than that. The key is the existence of the River Ure Navigation. 10¼ miles in length the Navigation was completed in 1773. Its greater part was formed from the natural course of the River Ure but there were cuts – canalised sections with locks – at Milby and at Newby. The final two miles was a canal that branched off the River Ure on the edge of Ripon. The crucial fact is that the Navigation was bought by the L&T.

It is arguable that, in buying the Navigation, the L&T intended to attract goods traffic from Boroughbridge towards Ripon where it could be transhipped to its line. The GNE could compete by building a branch to Boroughbridge. Moreover, it could attract goods traffic from Ripon to Boroughbridge by the Navigation, the reverse of the flow possibly envisaged by the L&T. Evidence for this theory is provided by the fact that, under the powers of its 1846 Act, the GNE bought a strip of land from the edge of its Boroughbridge station to the side of Milby Cut.

The route of the Pilmoor and Boroughbridge Act of 1846 was similar to the first part of the GNE's 1844 Harrogate branch project. From Pilmoor the branch ran straight for four of its 5¾ miles. At Milby, just outside Boroughbridge,

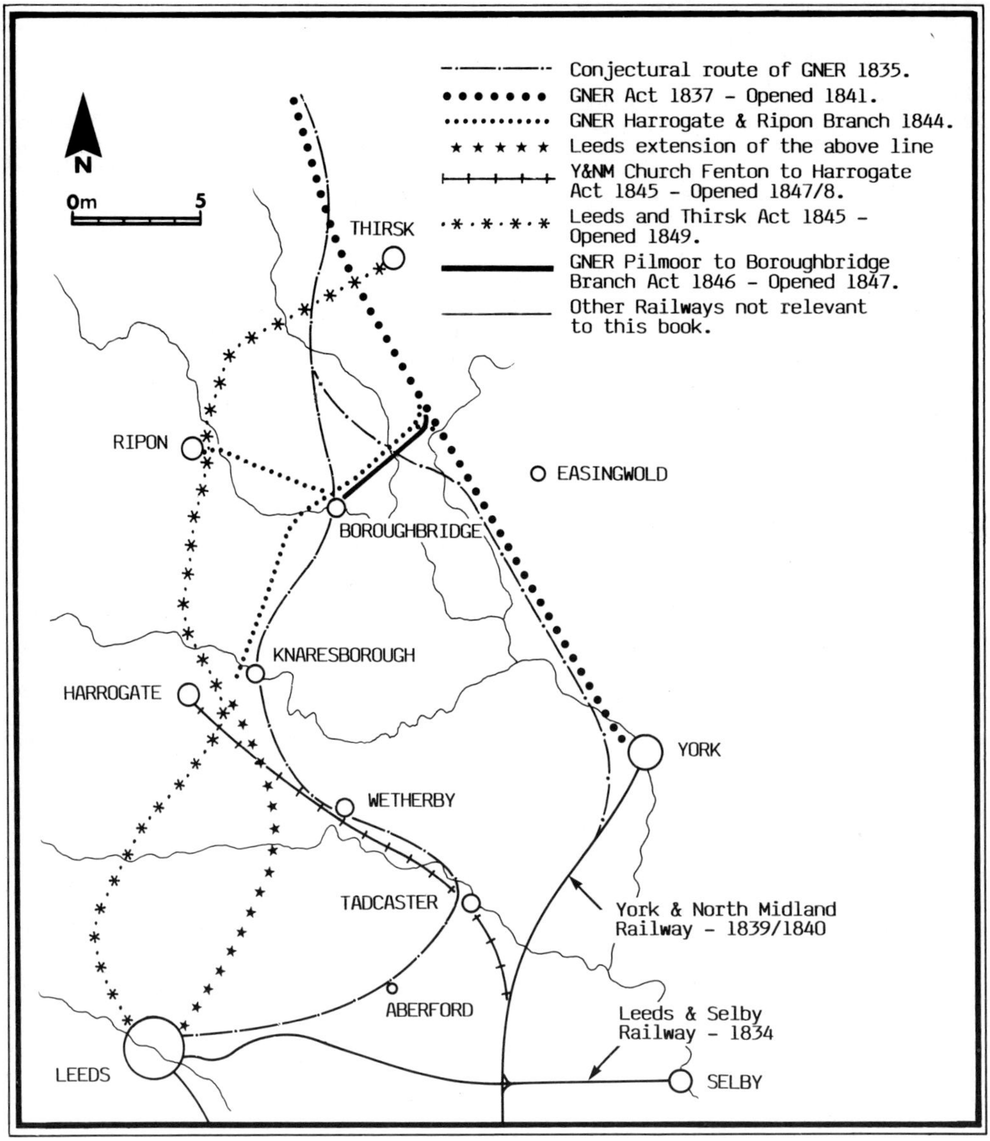
Conjectural route of GNER 1835.
GNER Act 1837 - Opened 1841.
GNER Harrogate & Ripon Branch 1844.
Leeds extension of the above line
Y&NM Church Fenton to Harrogate Act 1845 - Opened 1847/8.
Leeds and Thirsk Act 1845 - Opened 1849.
GNER Pilmoor to Boroughbridge Branch Act 1846 - Opened 1847.
Other Railways not relevant to this book.
N
0m
5
THIRSK
RIPON
EASINGWOLD
BOROUGHBRIDGE
KNARESBOROUGH
HARROGATE
YORK
WETHERBY
TADCASTER
York & North Midland Railway - 1839/1840
ABERFORD
Leeds & Selby Railway - 1834
LEEDS
SELBY

curves took the line to its terminus adjacent to Milby Cut.

The 1846 Act also included a southern curve at Pilmoor, enabling trains from Boroughbridge to go north or south once they reached the main line. Although the southern curve remained an intention for some years, it was never built.

The Pilmoor to Boroughbridge branch was opened on June 17th 1847. No contemporary records of the line's construction have been discovered by the author. The only record of the line at the time of its opening is the report of the Inspector for the Commissioners of Railways. The report is dated two days after the line opened, although the inspection itself was five days earlier:

Sir *19 June 1847*

I have to report for the information of the Commissioners of Railways that on the 14th inst. I inspected the Boroughbridge branch of the York and Newcastle Railway, the notices of completion having been given by the Company.

I was accompanied by Mr J. Stephenson the Resident Engineer and Mr Plews one of the Directors.

The branch commences at the Sessay station of the York and Newcastle Railway. It has but one curve of 40 chains radius, the remainder being almost a straight line to Boroughbridge, the total length being 5 miles 66 chains.

The gradients are practically level, one plain of 70 chains at 1 in 264 being the severest inclination upon it.

The cuttings and embankments are light, the greatest portion of the branch runs almost on the surface. The deepest cutting is 31 feet through sandy gravel. The highest embankment is 27 feet. They form slopes of 1½ to 1 and shew no tendency to slip.

There is one bridge over the line consisting of three oblique arches 30 feet span on the square, 33 feet on the skew, angle 63 degrees. The piers and abutments are freestone ashlar; the arches have ashlar facings and the body in brickwork turned in cement. The foundation is strong and the bridge is a handsome and substantial structure.

The River Swale is to be crossed by a bridge having three arches of 50-feet span. This bridge is incomplete. The abutments and piers are built up to the springing course but the arches are not yet commmenced. A temporary wooden viaduct has been erected alongside the bridge for the passage of the trains until its completion, which is not expected before the end of the summer. The viaduct is rough but strong and well put together. It is similar in principle and detail to those now existing between Darlington and Newcastle whose sufficiency has been proved. There is but a single line over it and two sharp curves at each end leading to it. The passing through the points and the curves at each end requires a very moderate speed which ensures the viaduct from any risk. I passed a heavy train of coal wagons above 200 tons over it and it was firm.

There are 2 small cattle passages under the line not exceeding 12-foot openings. They are crossed by flat iron girders each of which has been proved to 20 tons.

The stations are Brafferton   3½ miles
                  Boroughbridge 5¾ miles
The buildings and platforms were erected and available and the signals up. A turntable at Boroughbridge capable of turning an engine was complete.

The curves and gradients do not differ from the Parliamentary plans and sections beyond the limits authorised by Parliament.

The permanent way is double throughout except the short distance over the temporary viaduct. It is in all aspects similar to that on the York and Newcastle Railway, competently laid and ballasted and in good working order.

I am not aware of anything affecting public safety which should prevent this branch from being opened to traffic. I am, Sir, your very obedient servant.

Captain R.E. Waddington   Inspector of Railways

Several items from the report deserve comment:

Firstly, the reference to the line starting at Sessay station should have been to Pilmoor. In 1847 there was no station at Pilmoor, for there was no habitation at Pilmoor for a station to serve. Brafferton was 2½ miles from Pilmoor rather than the 3½ miles stated.

Secondly, according to the report there was a turntable at Boroughbridge. There was no turntable at Pilmoor, although one was considered in the early years, but there were turntables at Thirsk and Darlington. After the early years trains from Boroughbridge rarely went beyond Pilmoor and, as tank engines were normally used, the turntable at Boroughbridge may have been removed. A detailed plan of the station in 1865 does not show a turntable.

Thirdly, when it was opened in 1847 the line was double. This fact is obvious from the formation that existed until final closure, with the remaining single line at one side of what was enough space for a double line. An Ordnance Survey map of 1852 indicates that the line was by then single. Presumably it was realised that the traffic potential of the line did not justify a double track and the second one was removed soon after opening.

Lastly, with regard to the 'rough but strong' temporary wooden viaduct over the River Swale, there is a further reference in Section 4 of this book.

No account of any opening festivities has been seen by the author. A Boroughbridge historian commented in 1853 that: "By means of this line . . . Boroughbridge is placed in communication with all parts of the country. This grand steam revolution was a heavy loss to Boroughbridge. The posting establishments became useless and had to be sold off, and the number of inns, once scarcely equal to the entertainment of the shoals of travellers, became too many by half for the wants of the place".

1848 – 1875

The line from Pilmoor to Boroughbridge having been opened in 1847, the possibility of an extension southwards was revived in 1848, even though in the event 29 years were to pass before it was opened. The first plan was a Bill published in 1848 by the Y&NM for a line from Boroughbridge to Harrogate. Its route started at Boroughbridge station with an end-on connection with the line from Pilmoor. It continued southwards past Minskip and Ferrensby, and on through Knaresborough alongside the planned East and West Yorkshire Junction (E&WJ) line from York. Reaching Starbeck, the route continued in a south-westerly direction parallel to Hookstone Road before swinging to the north and joining the Y&NM's Church Fenton to Harrogate line very close to its terminus at the now long-closed Brunswick station. The orientation of the line was into Harrogate from the south. Any train that was to continue southwards would have had to reverse at Brunswick station.

The 1848 plan suffered the same fate as many other branches at the time, due to the collapse of the money market and the disgrace of George Hudson. Nothing more happened to the Boroughbridge to Knaresborough plans until 1865.

In autumn that year a new company, the Leeds, North Yorkshire and Durham Railway (LNYD), proposed a line through the heartland of what was by then the North Eastern Railway (NER). The history of the LNYD is bound up with the attempts by the London and North Western Railway (LNW) to gain access to NER territory, in particular to the River Tees and to Scarborough. The LNW already had a line that entered Leeds from the west via Huddersfield. From Leeds the LNYD's route was through Chapeltown, Wetherby, Easingwold, Helmsley and up Bilsdale to the River Tees and on to West Hartlepool. There was a branch eastwards from Helmsley to Kirbymoorside, Pickering and Scarborough as well as several other branches and connecting lines.

The NER had its own routes from Leeds to Scarborough and to the River Tees, and vigorously opposed the LNYD. Several of the more influential of the promoters of the LNYD were persuaded to abandon their support; the NER paid their Parliament expenses and promised to supply the areas to be served by the LNYD with NER-sponsored lines. The LNYD Bill was defeated in Parliament.

As part of its response to the LNYD the NER proposed several new lines whose effect would have been to create a completely new route from Leeds to Scarborough, bypassing York and going instead via Wetherby, Harrogate, Knaresborough, Boroughbridge, Coxwold and Old Malton (see map). The company was authorised to construct them all.

These proposals included the line from Boroughbridge to Knaresborough and a link from the Pilmoor to Boroughbridge branch to the Thirsk and Malton branch, crossing over the GNE main line by a bridge. But again, in the same way as nearly twenty years earlier, nothing happened for several years. Eventually construction of the Boroughbridge to Knaresborough line was started. The link across the GNE main line at Pilmoor was built but was never used.

As with the Pilmoor to Boroughbridge line, there are records neither of the construction of the line nor of its opening. Once again the report of the Board of Trade Inspector, C.J. Hutchinson, provides the only contemporary record, of which the following are extracts:

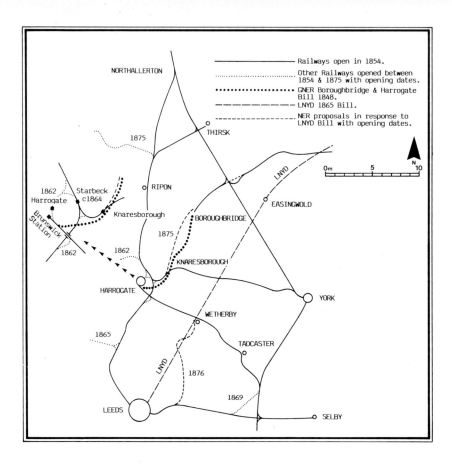

Railways open in 1854.
.... Other Railways opened between 1854 & 1875 with opening dates.
●●●●●●●●● GNER Boroughbridge & Harrogate Bill 1848.
———— LNYD 1865 Bill.
– – – – NER proposals in response to LNYD Bill with opening dates.

Railway Department
Board of Trade
29 March 1875

Sir,

I have the honour to report for the information of the Board that . . . I have inspected the Knaresborough and Boroughbridge line of the North Eastern Railway. This line which is single throughout, with the exception of loops and sidings at Boroughbridge, Staveley and Knaresborough Junction, is 7 miles 21 chains in length. It commences with a junction with the York and Knaresborough Railway, near to Knaresborough, and terminates with a junction with the line from Pilmoor Junction to Boroughbridge. New stations have been constructed at Staveley and Boroughbridge. The land has been purchased and the overbridges constructed for a double line.

The steepest gradient on the line has an inclination of 1 in 100 and the sharpest curve a radius of 20 chains.

The permanent way is of the usual description as employed on the North Eastern Railway. There are three bridges over the railway (largest span 33 ft) constructed entirely of masonry. Under the line there are 19 bridges all being brick or stone abutments and spanned with brick arches or cast or wrought iron girders, the largest spans being respectively 40ft, 30ft and 50ft. There is also a viaduct of two spans of 125ft each over the River Ure, in which wrought iron girders resting on cast iron columns have been employed. These bridges appear to have been all substantially constructed and to be standing well. In the case of the iron underbridges and the viaduct the theoretical strength is sufficient and the amount of deflection beneath a rolling load of engines moderate.

There are no public level crossings and no tunnels on the line.

The fencing is of post and rail.

(Staveley was the original name for Copgrove station.)

The Inspector decreed that, until the link over the GNE main line to the Thirsk and Malton branch was completed, the entire line from Pilmoor to Knaresborough, together with that from Pilmoor to Pickering via Coxwold and Gilling, be worked with tank engines. As noted above, the link never was completed but locomotives other than tank engines did work over both lines.

The Boroughbridge to Knaresborough line was opened on April 1st 1875. It commenced with a junction with the line from Pilmoor a short distance from the original Boroughbridge station, which became the goods station. A new passenger station was erected on the new line.

The line climbed by an embankment towards the bridge over the River Ure, high enough to give adequate clearance to commercial craft using the river. It continued in a straight line, dropping down to the River Tutt and finally climbing over the watershed between the Rivers Ure and Nidd. It made a junction with the York to Harrogate line east of the tunnel at Knaresborough station.

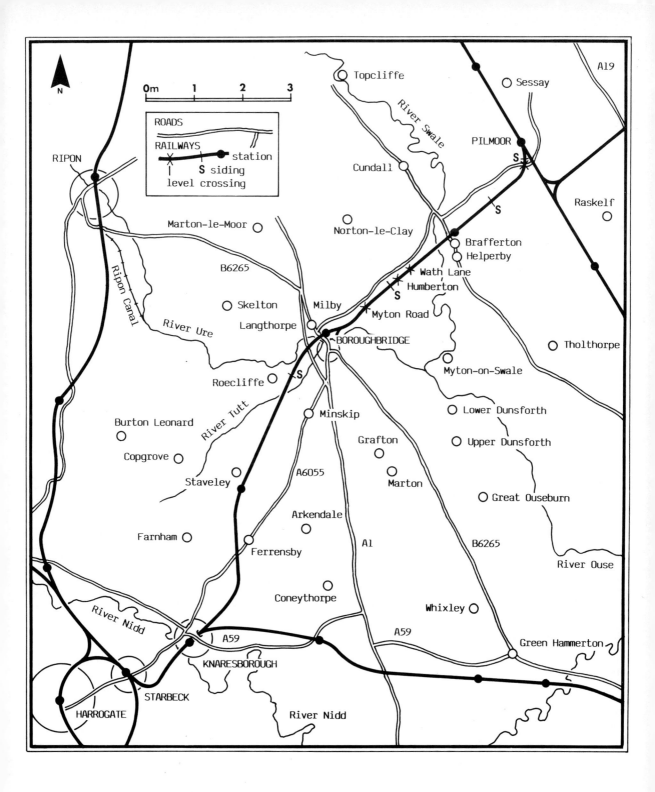

N

0m 1 2 3

ROADS
RAILWAYS
S siding
level crossing

× station

RIPON

Topcliffe

Sessay

A19

River Swale

PILMOOR

S

Cundall

Raskelf

S

Marton-le-Moor

Norton-le-Clay

Brafferton

Helperby

B6265

Wath Lane

Humberton

Ripon Canal

Skelton

Milby

S

Myton Road

Tholthorpe

River Ure

Langthorpe

BOROUGHBRIDGE

Myton-on-Swale

Roecliffe

S

River Tutt

Minskip

Lower Dunsforth

Burton Leonard

Grafton

Upper Dunsforth

Copgrove

A6055

Marton

Staveley

Great Ouseburn

Arkendale

A1

B6265

Farnham

Ferrensby

River Ouse

River Nidd

Coneythorpe

Whixley

A59

A59

Green Hammerton

KNARESBOROUGH

STARBECK

HARROGATE

River Nidd

2 Pilmoor

When the Great North of England Railway (GNE) was opened in 1841 there was nothing at Pillmoor (as it was spelled at the time). Contemporary maps show mostly moorland, but with patches of woodland and a few farms. The area through which the GNE ran is shown as Jobbing Cross, a name of obscure origin.

There was no station at Pilmoor even when the Pilmoor to Boroughbridge branch was opened in 1847, if the Bradshaw timetable is to be believed. The evidence of this timetable suggests – no more – that the branch trains ran to and from Sessay or even Thirsk. By 1849 there was a station and thereafter most branch trains shuttled between Boroughbridge and Pilmoor.

Pilmoor station had three platforms: two on the main line and one on the branch. The main station buildings were on the northbound, or down, platform. The original junction signalbox was at the northern end of the down platform, in the angle between the main line and the branch. However a new box was built in 1903 on the opposite side of the main line, at the northern end of the southbound, or up, platform. Over the years this box was variously known as Pilmoor Junction, Pilmoor and, from 1943, Pilmoor North.

From 1841, when the GNE was opened, until 1942 there were two main line tracks through the station. An up siding to the north converged onto the main line at the north end of the up platform. In 1942 this siding was converted into an up slow line from Thirsk to Pilmoor. In the same year a down slow line was installed through the station. As the station buildings were in the way they were demolished. A new station building and a separate station master's house were built. The station master, Mr Rex, and his family moved to a temporary timber house nearby until their new home was ready. Finally the up slow line was extended southwards through the station to Alne in 1959; by this time the station was completely closed.

Although the Boroughbridge branch was double when first built, it was single for most of its life. Normal NER practice was for single lines to be doubled where they made a junction with a double line. This was the case at Knaresborough, at the southern end of the branch, but there is some uncertainty about Pilmoor. An 1852 Ordnance Survey map shows a single line connection with the main line but there is a reference in the NER's 1875 working timetables to 'West Junction' at Pilmoor. Moreover the official railway name for the cottages at the Pilmoor gatehouse, half a mile down the branch from the station, was 'Inner Junction cottages'. These both suggest that the single line was doubled for its junction with the main line, but there is no reference in any of the NER books and papers to a signalbox at an Inner Junction or West Junction. This remains a mystery.

Operationally Pilmoor was unusual. The junction signalbox was equivalent to two quite separate boxes. It could be open for trains on the Boroughbridge branch but without any involvement whatever with main line trains. In these circumstances it was 'switched out', and the signalboxes to the south and north controlled the main line.

Over the years through trains between the main line and the branch were infrequent. Between 1867 and 1875 there was a passenger train between Boroughbridge and Thirsk, and in the late 1930s the branch goods pickup worked onto the main line (see Section 10). Southbound trains from the main line onto the branch had to reverse from the up main line to the down and then run forward into the branch.

Albert Clemit was a porter signalman at Pilmoor from 1938 and was intimate with its workings:

There was a lot of transferring of horseboxes from main line trains to Brafferton, Boroughbridge, Copgrove or Starbeck, and vice versa. When a train from York to Newcastle had anything for the branch, it wasn't necessary for you to open Pilmoor Junction signalbox to the main line. The movement was all on one side of the main line – the down side. All you did was go into the cabin and pull the points over and fetch him back into the branch siding, leaving the horsebox in there for the Harrogate engine to pick up. Then the loco would come out again, back onto his train and set off. The Harrogate engine would put it into the rear of his train.

Coming from the north the train stopped on the up main line. The engine backed the wagon for the branch into the up siding, came out of the siding to his train and away. When a branch train came from Harrogate I'd have to open the signalbox up and its engine seesawed across the main line to collect the wagon.

Sometimes Harrogate trains would bring a vehicle that was to go through to York. First the engine would run round in the loop on the branch at Pilmoor station. Then it would propel out onto the main line, cross from the down to the up main, run forward to the points and back into the up siding. Then we had to detach the loco on a parcels train, back into the up siding and fetch the wagon out. As porter signalman, I had to do the shunting and work the signalbox.

At this time the Boroughbridge branch pickup ran through to Thirsk. On the way back it would have to seesaw across from the up main to the down main and then onto the branch. If it was too busy to get him across straight away we used to back him into the up siding to get him out of the way.

Initially Pilmoor was an interchange station between the main line and the Boroughbridge branch. This role was enhanced when the Thirsk and Malton branch was opened in 1853. As an interchange station conditions there were bleak. Not until 1861 were passengers waiting on the up, York-bound, platform provided with a shelter. And it was not until 1883 that this was converted into a proper waiting room with a door.

Pilmoor was the site of an unsuccessful experiment in station lighting. 'Oil gas apparatus' was installed there in 1896. Gas was manufactured from the oil and stored in a small gasometer at one end of a retort house. However, in 1905 the NER replaced the apparatus with conventional oil lighting.

Although the station was not intended for the scattered community around Pilmoor, people from the surrounding area did try to use it. In 1859 there was a complaint of trespass by people making their way across the fields to the station. In 1860 Sir William Gallwey of Pilmoor Hall approached the NER with a proposition to build a 'refreshment house' at the station with a road to it. The NER replied that, if he would make the road, the Company would make a footpath along the side of the railway line and would allow people to use it on payment of one shilling (5p) per annum. This must have been too hard a bargain for Sir William, for neither the refreshment house nor the road were made.

In 1889, the Gallwey family in the shape of Captain Paine-Gallwey once more asked the NER to make a 650-yard long road to the station. And once again the NER refused, conceding only that if others made the road the Company might contribute towards the cost. In 1896, for the final time, the residents applied again and the Company repeated that the work should be carried out by the local authority or residents and that it would consider whether to assist in the cost.

There never was any road access to Pilmoor station and it remained an interchange station all its life. However, it was used by the railway staff and their families who lived in the cottages south of Jobbing Cross bridge, and for whom in

1879 the NER had made a footpath alongside the main line from the bridge to the station.

This book is not the place to relate the story of the community at Pilmoor. Suffice to say that there were seventeen dwellings, excluding farms; there was a church, a reading room, a shop, and what we of the late twentieth century would describe as a 'community spirit'.

Pilmoor's first station master may have been a Mr Potts. Certainly he was there in 1854, although he is variously described as station clerk and station master. In 1855 a Mr Ness complained to the NER of having been left behind by a train at Pilmoor through the neglect, as he put it, of Mr Potts. The NER rejected the complaint. Indeed they shewed their confidence in Mr Potts by increasing his salary from 20 shillings (£1) to 23 shillings (£1.15) per week, until he was provided with a house. However, only a few months later Mr Potts was moved to Sessay station.

It was not until 1854 that a station house was built, together with a waiting room. The house was altered in 1857 and again in 1865. The 1865 problem appears to have been serious: the NER minute refers to 'the unhealthy state of Pilmoor station master's house'. Again in 1866 there were complaints about the unhealthy state of the house. Thomas Prosser, the NER's architect, was instructed to submit a plan for making it sanitarily inhabitable.

The station building was enlarged and improved several times before it was demolished in 1942 to make way for the widening of the main line. The new house was built to a standard LNER design and, unlike its predecessor, not on the station platform but set back in its own grounds.

Problems with the drinking water at Pilmoor station persisted for many years. But water for other purposes was abundant. Oswald Gillery, whose father was station master during the 1930s, recalls:

There were two sources of water for the station: there were two huge rainwater butts which collected water from the station roof and piped it into the kitchen, and the huge underground lake that was rumoured to be there. If you lifted a floorboard at the station you could see water standing under the floor. There was a pump and it was the porter's job to pump water into a tank for the station toilet. A pipe from this tank also led into the house. Drinking water came in large cans from a pump at Brafferton station and was emptied into a big reservoir tank in our pantry.

Saturday night was bath night and at about ten to eight my father used to tell us to get ready. He would get the zinc bath out, put it in front of the fire in the living room and fill it with cold water. A train from Harrogate arrived at about 8.10pm and left at 8.50pm. The engine used to run round the train and back onto the other end, so that it was always just outside our door. As soon as the engine got backed onto the train my father was out with two big buckets. He would put them under the injector pipe and fill them with scalding water. My brother and I would get bathed and my mother and father after us, filling up with hot water from the engine each time.

As Pilmoor was mainly an interchange station tickets sales were not great: an average of 14 a day in 1895, down to 7 a day in 1940. Most of this business must have been railway staff and families. The figures do not include passengers changing trains and the station was busier than they suggest.

Pilmoor's goods facilities were rudimentary. It had no station yard, no coal depot, no goods warehouse, no weighbridge, but it did have a siding from the very first years until the last. It diverged from the Boroughbridge branch about 200 yards from the station and passed through a gate onto 'the Moor'.

Originally the Moor siding led across the Jobbing Cross

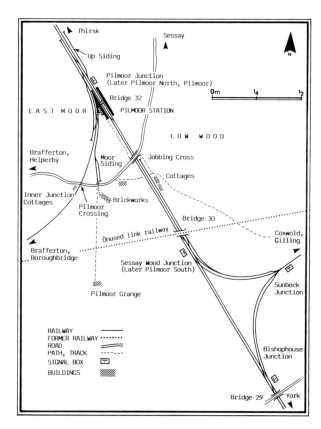

road to Baines's brick and tile works. When the works was first opened is not known to the author but a siding to it is shown on an 1852 Ordnance Survey map. In 1868 the Goods Manager of the NER complained that "(the siding) is said to be so much out of gauge as to be unsafe for an engine to go into. I presume that the proper plan will be for you to put it into proper repair and to charge Sir William Gallwey with the cost." The reply is not known but the siding was probably closed at about this time. It was cut back to finish at the Jobbing Cross road. Later a second parallel siding was installed. These were Pilmoor's goods yard and, unlike the station proper, they had road access. The brickworks itself remained open for many years thereafter; in 1890 it was owned by Mr J.W. Green, who also had the Roecliffe brickworks (see Section 6).

The Moor siding was used by local farmers for loading agricultural produce, including grain, potatoes and sugar beet. Timber from the woods was loaded there too. During the first World War Franks of Pickering pulled out a lot of timber for pit props. The peak year was 1915. In 1918 Job Earnshaw and Brothers contracted with the NER to load timber in the siding that was an extension of the Pilmoor station run-round loop. The main clause of the agreement was that loading should take place on Sundays only when there were no trains on the branch, with the full wagons being taken away on the Monday morning.

As well as the Moor siding there was another at the railway cottages half a mile south of Pilmoor station. The main function of this siding was to enable a slow train to be shunted off the double track main line, to make way for a faster train coming up behind. But at its buffer end it was also used for receiving wagons of coal for the eleven railway dwellings alongside.

Pilmoor station's decline was hastened when trains on the Gilling, Helmsley and Malton lines increasingly ran to York or made connections with the main line at Raskelf or Alne rather than at Pilmoor; these trains ceased using Pilmoor in the early 1930s. The closure to passengers of the Boroughbridge branch in September 1950 sounded its death knell. Nevertheless the station continued to serve the needs of the dwindling railway community and the few nearby farms until May 5th 1958. It was closed to goods on September 14th 1959.

Pilmoor North signalbox, as it was then known, was closed on May 15th 1960. It was replaced by a ground frame that gave access to a 500-yard length of the Boroughbridge branch that was retained as a siding after the complete closure of the line between Pilmoor and Brafferton in 1950.

What of Pilmoor station today? All traces of the signalbox and the up platform have disappeared. On the down side the platform has all but disappeared but the 1942 station house remains, as does the retort house for the unsuccessful 1896 experiment in oil gas lighting.

A class B16 locomotive heads a goods train south through Pilmoor c1949. Pilmoor North signalbox is in the centre background; the Boroughbridge branch and platform disappear off to the left. (map ref. 463733)
(J.W. Hague, courtesy of David Beeken)

Looking south at Pilmoor station c1949, with the East Coast Main Line (left) and the Boroughbridge branch (right). The 1942 station master's house is centre and the retort house for the 1896 experiment in oil gas lighting is right foreground. The Moor siding can be seen diverging from the branch.
(J.W. Hague, courtesy of David Beeken)

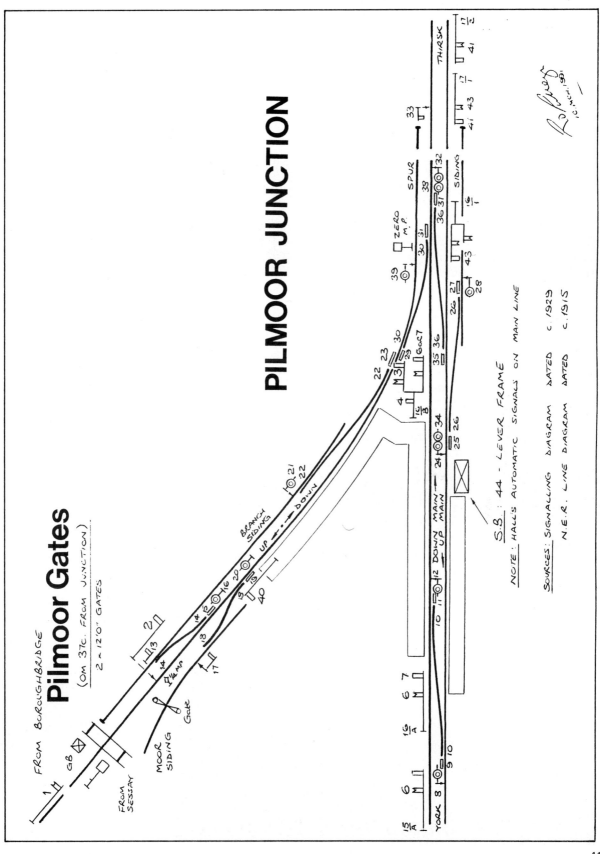

PILMOOR JUNCTION

Pilmoor Gates

(ON 3½c. FROM JUNCTION)

2 × 12'0" GATES

S.B.: 44 - LEVER FRAME

NOTE: HALL'S AUTOMATIC SIGNALS ON MAIN LINE

SOURCES: SIGNALLING DIAGRAM   DATED   c. 1929

N.E.R. LINE DIAGRAM   DATED   c. 1915

11

Sequence at Pilmoor at about 1800 on May 30th 1950. Class V2 locomotive 60933 on the 1735 York to Darlington local service, connecting with the 1700 from Harrogate; class G5 67337 on the 1700 from Harrogate, waiting to form the 1816 back; class A4 locomotive 60002 "Sir Murrough Wilson" approaching with the 1335 Edinburgh-Kings Cross express.
(Chris Wilson)

The zero post marking the precise commencement of the Boroughbridge branch at Pilmoor.
(J.W. Hague courtesy of David Beeken)

Pilmoor Gatehouse

Half a mile down the Boroughbridge branch from Pilmoor station there was the first of the four level crossings between Pilmoor and Boroughbridge. There were two cottages adjoining the crossing, known as 'Inner Junction cottages'. The crossing keeper lived in the nearer, no. 2, and a railway worker lived in the further, no. 1.

No. 1 has been occupied by the same family since 1907, when Herbert Turner, track walker, platelayer and, later, ganger moved there with his family. Mr Turner died in 1980, aged 104. His granddaughter, Dorothy Turner, lives to this day in the house that is now a combination of both the original dwellings.

Mrs Eleanor Watson lived in no. 2 cottage as the gate-keeper at Pilmoor from 1935 until the line between Pilmoor and Brafferton was closed in 1950. Her husband, Bob Watson, was a ganger on the Pilmoor to Brafferton length:

My gates were supposed to be closed across the roadway all the time, even when no trains were coming, except at night. That was the rule. There weren't even small gates at the side, so that I had to open the gates even for bicycles. There were a lot of cycles in those days and I usually had the gates open to the road to let them through, even though it was really against the rules. An inspector used to come down once a month to sign the book in a little hut next to the levers. Sometimes I didn't know when he was coming and he would find the gates open to the road: 'Oh you must abide by the rules Mrs Watson.'

The local hunt used to meet near Pilmoor church. One day one of the redcoats, who seemed to be the master of the hunt, came up and was very cross because the gates were closed against them. There was a train coming but he thought that the train should be held up for the hunt. They couldn't see the train because of the bend in the line towards Brafferton. He reported me to York but I never heard any more about it.

Occasionally, I didn't hear the bell that said that there was a train coming, as I was in the garden and I had to dash out and close the gates. The engine drivers were quite good and very nice. They used to stop and, after I closed the gates, they came on.

During the War the baker used to come from Helperby. Food was rationed and there were bread units; you could only have maybe one or two loaves. The baker didn't go to individual houses and, if the people in the railway cottages and farms round about wanted any bread, they used to bring their bread units to me at the gatehouse and I got the bread for them. Then they would come and collect it from me later in the day. In those days we got 13 buns for 1s (5p).

On the closure of the stretch of line between Pilmoor and Brafferton permanent fences were erected across the railway on each side of the crossing. The line was taken up not many weeks later. Today the two cottages still stand, now joined into the one residence.

Class G5 locomotive 1915 passes Pilmoor crossing in the late 1930s, with a train to Harrogate. The "Gate Stop Board" is part of the 1936 signalling scheme (see section 11). (MR 462727).
(courtesy of Dorothy Turner)

Passenger train passing Pilmoor crossing to Harrogate, date unknown. The original "revolving board signal" for the crossing is on the right.
(courtesy of Dorothy Turner)

Brafferton

From Pilmoor the branch ran straight towards Borough-bridge across completely flat terrain. 2¼ miles from Pilmoor it pierced a ridge and reached the River Swale near the twin villages of Helperby and Brafferton. The road from the two villages to Cundall and Topcliffe runs along the ridge; it crossed the railway by the three-arched stone bridge described by Captain Waddington at the time of the opening of the line (Section 1).

Brafferton station, named after the nearer of the two villages, was partly inside and partly outside the cutting through the ridge. When the line was first opened it was double, and the station therefore possessed two platforms. On the abandonment of the second track one platform was made redundant.

A long drive led from the Brafferton to Cundall road into the station yard. A siding curved round the back of the yard to the loading dock on the right; the station building was on the left. Beyond the siding there was a 10-ton weighbridge and a small office. Intending passengers descended from the approach road to the station platform by a gravelled ramp at the southern end of the station building. The ramp ended on the platform alongside a lock-up shed that was erected in 1877 for storing parcels for delivery in the surrounding area. Prior to 1936 the station's signals and points were operated from a large wooden 'cupboard' on the platform, with nine working levers and three spares.

At the northern end of the station building there were the station coal house and a row of sleeper buildings with zinc tops. These contained a "stick house" where kindling was chopped up, the lamp room where paraffin was kept, and at the end the porters' room where there was a stove and where the staff ate their meals. At this end of the station there were a dozen steps from the platform up into the yard.

The main building was a large one. The ground floor contained the station offices and the station master's residence. For the station master the main entrance hall from the station yard led to a dining room and an adjacent kitchen with a walk-in pantry, all with flagstone floors. Also on the ground floor there were a general waiting room and a combined booking office and station master's office. In the waiting room there was a parcels weighing machine and two benches. The office contained the signalling block instruments as well as the many materials for the commercial life of the station: tickets, luggage labels, books of instructions, circulars.

Stairs led from the entrance hall to the first floor landing and the sitting room which had windows on three sides and gave extensive views to the north and east. Next to the sitting room there was a bedroom and, on the right at the head of the stairs the main bedroom. An extension, put up in 1893, provided a third bedroom.

Downstairs, the 1893 extension created a ladies' waiting room and toilet, and a gents' urinal and toilet. It also contained a single storey area for the station master with a small flagstone yard, wash house, privy, coal and ash stores.

Victorians appear to have had problems with basic hygiene. There were problems at Pilmoor, at Copgrove and at Brafferton. At the last-named the gents' urinal of 1893 was placed directly over the well from which the house's domestic water was supplied. In later years, when the significance of the juxtaposition of urinal and well was appreciated, the water from the well was condemned.

The station had its own station master for most of its 117-year life, with possibly only three during the first 81 years. For several years, like many small stations, it was placed under the control of another station, in this case Boroughbridge. It was controlled by Boroughbridge for the last nine years of its life.

Mrs Amy Pratt, the widow of Raymond Pratt who was station master from 1938 until 1946, has very clear memories of moving to Brafferton in 1938:

We came from Cross Gates (outside Leeds) to Brafferton and, unlike the house at Cross Gates, the one at Brafferton

Brafferton station in April 1949 looking approximately north east. The "Station Board", part of the 1936 signalling scheme (see section 11), is at the far end of the platform. (MR 438707)
(© John Armstrong/ courtesy of the John Armstrong Trustees)

Brafferton station looking towards Boroughbridge, shortly before final closure in 1964.
(author)

had nothing – no electricity, no gas and no running water. We packed up our vacuum cleaners and all the other things that worked off electricity, and we put them away. My husband applied to the Electricity Board to have the electricity brought from the village to the station but it would have cost £800, which was a lot of money in the 1930s. When we moved from Brafferton to Sleights, we got all the electrical things out again.

We had a very good kitchen garden down beyond the goods yard. At the bottom of the yard there was a big field that we also used. My husband was friendly with the local farmers and they ploughed it up for him. During the War we had it full of vegetables but we didn't want for food with all those farmers about. On the right-hand side of the drive down to the station we had another garden with roses and various other things.

It was a good-sized house and we paid very little rent for it. It had a good kitchen and a big dining room on the ground floor. The sitting room had a lovely view over the White Horse and the Moors. We often used to stand and look out at the view.

We had a well with a semi-rotary pump to get the water into the bathroom tank. My husband used to do the pumping but so did anybody who came into the house. I remember so well that when we arrived at Sleights I turned the tap on and the water came out without having to be pumped up into the tank first. I was so thrilled! Water was heated by the boiler in the kitchen. It was calor gas for lighting and coal ovens for cooking. It was all very primitive but it never seemed to bother me.

My husband was very keen on model railways. He and our son Keith had a marvellous model railway in an old railway goods van body on the bank opposite the station, on what had been the old platform when it was a double line.

Over the years the number of other staff varied considerably. Until the end of the passenger service in 1950, as well as the station master there were always two porter signalmen and a clerk. These were augmented by one or more goods porters and extra clerks so that at busy times there mght be eight staff working full time at the station.

Even in its early years it can hardly be said that Brafferton station was well used by passengers, as can be seen in the figures in Appendix A: an average of 28 tickets sold per day in 1885, down to 13 per day in 1940. The figures show how it experienced the decline suffered by most country stations after the First World War.

The main local destinations were predominantly Knaresborough, Harrogate and York. To Knaresborough and Harrogate the journey was straightforward but passengers to York usually travelled via Pilmoor. The flow towards Pilmoor was always significant, especially for the first train in the morning.

Geoff Hockliffe was a user of the station during the late 1930s, attending Knaresborough Grammar School until 1941 when he started work.

In the late 1930s there were not many people from Brafferton on the first train to Harrogate. I was the only one that went to school from there, but there were several others from other stations on the line.

We who went to school on the train were very mischievous, and I often used to wonder why we weren't thrown off the trains. Coming out of the tunnel at Knaresborough there was the junction where the train Staff was handed by the signalman to the driver as it went onto the branch to Boroughbridge. One winter night we Grammar School lads took a load of snowballs in with us. We opened the carriage window and let fly at the signalman. I can see it now: one hitting the handrail and splattering his bald head! He had the train pulled up at Copgrove and had us all questioned. No-one admitted it, of course, but they knew very well that we had. They searched the train but they didn't see that we still had ample supplies of snowballs up on the luggage rack. I think they took it in good part, because we didn't do any real damage.

Our biggest mischief was when the trains were coming through the tunnel at Knaresborough. Usually in those days the trains didn't have compartments; occasionally we had the luxury of a corridor train and that's when we got up to this little piece of mischief. The girls got into one compartment and we boys were in the next one. Coming through the tunnel, which seemed a long one because the train was still accelerating out of Knaresborough station, we boys dashed through to where the girls were, ruffled their hair and gave them a kiss, and ran back to our compartment, all in the dark of the tunnel. Afterwards they used to come through, kicking up a fuss, although I think they really quite enjoyed it. However, one night when we did it, they didn't kick up a fuss. It transpired that an old lady had got in at the last minute, and heaven knows who had ruffled her hair and kissed her! When she got out at Copgrove she came up to our window 'I won't report it this time, but don't let it happen again.' She threatened to have us all expelled from the school. She was a sweet old thing really.

After leaving school I worked at Barclays Bank at Boroughbridge. I cycled everyday but occasionally if it was very bad weather I took the train. Or if there was a very strong head wind I would take my bike on the train. I think the single fare including the cycle was about ninepence ha'penny (4p) or elevenpence ha'penny (5p).

However it is for its goods traffic that Brafferton is most remembered by former staff. The coal depot had two lines with ten coal cells in each. Originally there was one siding only in the yard but a second one was added in 1874. The sidings held four and twelve wagons respectively. There was another long siding parallel to the main line leading towards Pilmoor, a residue of the original double line.

The goods yard was small and, as is obvious from the accompanying plan, working wagons in and out was not straightforward. All wagons for either of the two sidings in the yard had to be taken up onto the coal depot first. Members of staff had their own ways of doing this. A train usually approached from Boroughbridge. In one method the locomotive detached the wagons for Brafferton from the remainder of the train, drew forward and up onto the back coal depot line – the line furthest from the main line – and lowered them into the appropriate siding. Life was more complicated if there were already wagons in the yard that were part-loaded and had to be put back where they were, or when empties had to be removed, but the technique was basically simple.

In the other method a wire rope was used to pull the wagons for the station into the long siding parallel to the main line. The locomotive then went up the coal depot and down into the yard, and removed any wagons that were to go away. These were put onto the remainder of the train on the main line. The locomotive drew the wagons out of the long siding and pushed them up onto the back coal depot line, whence they were allowed to roll down into the yard.

Complications arose with shunting coal wagons onto the depot. Wagons were placed by one of two ways. One involved the use of the wire rope. The locomotive 'roped the wagon by': it ran up onto the far coal depot line, pulling the wagons onto the near depot line. The other method, always frowned upon, was by fly-shunting. The locomotive, with wagons for the depot attached, ran forward until it had gathered momentum. At the right moment the driver eased off until the coupling between the locomotive and the wagon became slack. The guard slipped the coupling. The driver accelerated and drew away from the wagons. As soon as the locomotive was clear of the siding points they were switched and the wagons rolled onto the coal depot. The most important thing was to get the wagons clear of the main line so that, if necessary, the locomotive could get behind them and push them up onto the depot.

Taking coal wagons off the depot was either done by using the wire rope to pull them off, or by the station staff using a pinch bar and rolling them down onto the main line, in both cases ensuring that they were behind the locomotive.

George Berriman was a porter signalman from 1942:

Shunting the yard wasn't that difficult as long as you were organised. However, we had one or two old guards and they

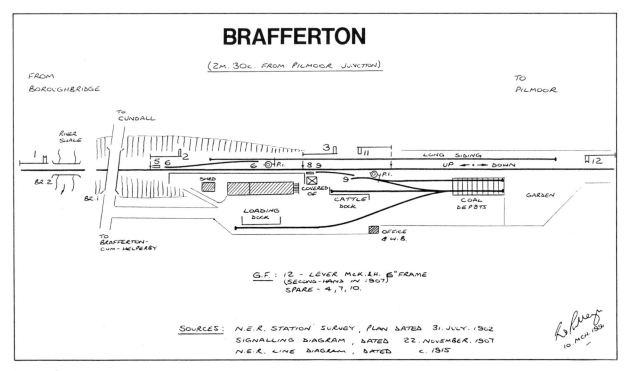

Class J39 locomotive 64855 shunting at Brafferton on May 17th 1958.
(Jim Sedgwick)

were as awkward as they could be. I knew the job and, if they shunted the yard in the way I said, it was all right. But one old chap wouldn't listen to me: 'I'm in charge of the train' he said. I let him carry on but he got tied in a knot. He was wasting his time and he was on bonus. Then eventually he came to me: 'I don't know how to move'. I'd already weighed up how to get out of it, so I said 'are you prepared to listen?' He was and so it didn't take long.

There were at least two shunting accidents at Brafferton. One took place in March 1911, when Goods Guard John Rodgers was injured. It happened while wagons were being roped by. The loop on the wagon side to which the rope was attached broke and Rodgers's hand was struck by the hook, breaking a bone. The Board of Trade report into the accident recommended that the method of working be altered. This was not done. In May 1933 there was another accident involving a rope. This time goods guard George Durham was injured when the rope suddenly became taut.

After shunting Brafferton yard the trains usually went on to Pilmoor where they reversed and returned. However they did sometimes reverse at Brafferton itself if there was no traffic for Pilmoor. As Brafferton had no section of double line for a locomotive to run round its train the wire rope was again used, either to rope the wagons into the long siding or onto the coal depot.

Keith Pratt, then the young son of station master Raymond Pratt, vividly recalls these movements onto and off the depot:

By design the depot was built to take locos and I can remember the notice 'ENGINES ARE ALLOWED ONTO THE DEPOTS'. Picture a small boy being able to go under the coal depot and look up to the underside of a steam loco!

During the First World War there was a 'remount depot' at Ramsden's farm at Myton-on-Swale, where horses were trained for hauling guns and any other function for which they were used in the army. Geoff Hockliffe's father was involved when they arrived at Brafferton station:

About 400 horses at a time came into Brafferton station. When a train was due in my Dad went round to get anyone that was available. Some were quite wild; others were broken in. Later mustangs from Canada were brought in. They'd ride one horse and have another at each side of it, and take them down the road to Myton. There were 48 men working at Myton on their training. The horses were there for about six weeks and then they went on their way to the Army. During the two years 9800 horses were trained. They went out by rail too. Horses were no longer needed after about 1916 and the remount depot was then closed.

The railway career of Frank Hick, later Chief Operating Manager of the North Eastern Region of BR, started at Brafferton in 1922 as a probationer clerk. Prior to that he had worked at Ramsden's farm at Myton:

The station master was Nathan Raw who was a real old-fashioned disciplinarian and who expected everything to be done right. Like most station masters in those days Mr Raw had a major concern about how much coal he could sell. Station masters always looked after the coal business themselves. I was never allowed to look after the coal statistics but I did weight the empty carts in and the full ones out.

One regular passenger to the station was the Prudential Insurance man. Nearly all the people in the local villages used to pay a penny or twopence a week insurance. The Prudential man came from Harrogate once a month to collect the premiums. He would get off the early train with his bicycle and he would cover villages like Helperby, Myton, Tholthorpe and others all around. In the evenings he would catch the six o'clock train back to Harrogate. As he sat in the waiting room waiting for the train back, you would hear him counting up his money.

From my previous employment I knew the farmers of the district and of course they took advantage of their knowledge of me. This included Ramsden's farm where I had previously worked and naturally they had an attitude towards me rather different from when I worked for them!

There was a local firm of seed merchants, T.N. Driffield and Sons. The seeds were sent in large sacks and most of them went by passenger train but with some by 'road wagons' on the goods trains. The seed went to almost every place in the kingdom.

Grain went out in railway sacks and the sack business was very important both to the farmers and to the railway. A railway sack would hold 12 stones of oats, 16 stones of barley and wheat or 18 stones of rye. 18 stones was too heavy for a man to lift off the ground so they had a machine. You wound a handle to lift the sack up to shoulder height, and the man took it onto his shoulders.

Potatoes also went out in private sacks from the potato merchants. The empty sacks came by rail in bundles. You knew that when these empty sacks came through to the farms there would be a big consignment of potatoes about a week later, which would need a wagon or wagons ordering. When the sacks were loaded they were despatched in wagons, or occasionally by passenger train like Driffield's seeds. There was a terrible wagon shortage in those days and the farmers simply couldn't get the wagons to load the potatoes and the grain. So to get a wagon for a farmer was quite a major job. You were in a key position because you could disarrange all their plans if they couldn't get, say, two ten-ton wagons or four five-ton wagons or even their 150 grain sacks. It was quite an organisation to meet their demands, like a game of dominoes. But we could juggle things around and usually get the right wagon for the right man at the right time.

Later, during the Second World War there were two goods porters, Charlie Buck and Queenie Whorley (née Tutt), as well as the two porter signalmen, George Berriman and Arthur Atkinson or, later, Benny Pawson. For Charlie Buck:

Brafferton was a rough place. We had barley and grain, potatoes, carrots. The grain went in the railway's 16-stone sacks and the potatoes in privately owned 8-stone sacks. From Ireland Driffield's used to get perennial rye grass seeds in sacks which weighed up to 22 stones. There was dried sugar beet pulp in bags too. The pulp was very light and they used to put eight stones in these huge bags.

Lifting sacks was a matter of a knack rather than brute force. On one occasion, for a bet, I carred 24 stones in three sacks. One was across my shoulders and two on top of that. There was a bit of bravado about that. George Berriman was a very slight chap but I've never known anyone carry a 16-stone sack easier. He was an artist.

We had some big jobs over the years. One of the biggest jobs was from the malt kiln in Helperby. They railed about 3000 tons of barley. On Tuesdays we loaded malt, about 30 tons, from the malt kiln which went to Kings Cross. 30 tons of potatoes went out every Monday for Drivers of Bradford. We had a big load of loose potatoes from the Ministry of Food that went to Germany to be made into starch. They had to be loaded loose in end-door wagons and then sprayed with purple dye. Then they had to be sheeted. When they arrived we found that some of these wagons still had two to three tons of coal left in them.

We used to load hay and straw in high-sided wagons. We could put 90 bales in a load. You filled the wagon body itself, then you put a layer on their edges and another layer on top, flat with a ridge down the middle. Then it was double sheeted, one from each end and tied in the middle. Reg Burton from Copgrove station used to come down to help us to load and he was an artist at sheeting. At odd times I had to do it on my own which was always a tremendous job. I didn't like sheeting.

We had a good trade in cattle coming in, thin ones for fattening unlike the ones that were sold from the market at Boroughbridge. Sometimes they came in on the pickup or sometimes on a special at 7 o'clock at night. On the specials they used to bring 70 to 100 cattle. With 10 to 12 in a wagon they came in up to eight wagons. You never had more wagons than you could accommodate in the yard, which was about eight.

When there was a load of cattle for a farm at Pilmoor they got Tommy Hartley from Boroughbridge with his cattle wagon to take them down. A farmer from Myton-on-Swale used to go over to Ireland to buy Irish cattle. Four or five wagon loads would come to Brafferton station from Ireland and they would then be walked along the road through Helperby to Myton. They used to come in as thin as anything and eat the grass as they walked along. They would get

Two views of Class J39 locomotive 64857 with the pickup approaching Brafferton from Boroughbridge on June 2nd 1951.   (Chris Wilson)

fattened up and became fine big beasts. Then they would be sold locally, being walked over Myton Pastures to Boroughbridge cattle market. Brian Driffield once had 40 ponies that came by rail.

The quotations above make no mention of the bomb dump near Brafferton that added to the workload of the staff at Brafferton during the Second World War. This is fully described in Section 12 of this book. All in all the goods traffic physically demanded much from the staff who handled it. The post of porter signalman was, as the name suggests, one that combined two functions. It was created for lines where there were too few trains to employ full-time signalmen. He signalled the trains when necessary but at other times he was on portering duties. On some lightly-used branch lines the portering duties predominated.

The station masters of small country stations were important people in an era when the station was a valued part of the local community. The station master himself supplied coal to many, if not to most, of the dwellings in the vicinity. Some station masters remained at one station for many years, because they had a particularly lucrative coal sale. Many were the talented station masters who, once they reached a station with a good coal business, lost ambition.

At some stations, and Brafferton is a good example, goods staff were difficult to recruit and to keep. In these circumstances the relationship between the station master and his staff was more relaxed than usual, perhaps to the regret of the station master. The story is told of Raymond Pratt, Brafferton station master during the War, who looked in at the porters' room one day and found a ganger with a railway sack round his shoulders and Ned Richmond, a platelayer, cutting his hair. The station master indicated his disapproval of cutting hair in the railway company's time. "It

grows in Company's time,'' came the ripost. The station master said ''Not all of it''. ''I'm not cutting all of it off!''

As with all country stations, decline set in after the Second World War. The first event was the withdrawal of the passenger service in 1950 and the line from beyond the station to Pilmoor was closed and removed. The remaining clerk's job was abolished but the station master and a porter remained. In 1955 the station was placed under the control of the Boroughbridge station master, Walter Watson. Charlie Buck was the only person left:

After Mr Hunsley, the last station master, left the station house was unoccupied and fell into disrepair. In the last years it was very quiet and the pickup didn't always come. One man could easily handle the traffic. Mr Watson, the station master, had the coal sale which was still a good one. He came to Brafferton by car on Tuesdays and Fridays. He used to leave £1 railway cash float and £1 coal money. Sometimes I would go and work somewhere else. Occasionally up to 50 old wagons were brought down for storage before being scrapped. The engine bringing the wagons down from Boroughbridge would rope them by and push them up the line towards Pilmoor; they might be there a fortnight or even three months.

Towards the end, the track was in a very poor state. We had derailments in the yard. We had an engine off in the yard two or three times. The sleepers were rotten and it was in a terrible state. Once we had a coal wagon that went clean over the end of the coal depot.

Along with the remainder of the branch, Brafferton was closed in October 1964. The track was removed some time later. The station house, in poor condition having had no occupant since 1955, quickly became derelict and was subsequently demolished.

4 River Swale Bridge, Three Gatehouses and Humberton Siding

A third of a mile past Brafferton the railway crossed the River Swale. As noted in Section 1, Captain Waddington visited the line shortly before its opening in 1847 and found the bridge to be incomplete. A temporary timber viaduct was in place alongside.

Five large timbers from the temporary viaduct still exist, embedded in the river bottom and protruding to a few inches below normal summer water level: permanent evidence of the temporary viaduct. For many years on hot summer days the youths of Helperby and Brafferton jumped or dived off the permanent bridge into the River Swale, taking care always to avoid the timbers on the downstream side.

The bridge is a graceful one of three semi-elliptical 55-foot arches, 262 feet in overall length. It is built of stone and, with a width of 23 feet 10 inches, it was quite clearly built for a double track railway. The parapets consisted of iron stanchions let into the coping stones, joined by wire ropes. The two piers are on the land, thus permitting movement along the river banks under the outer arches. The bridge still stands and appears sound, although the number of trees growing out of the stonework cannot be good for it.

Class G5 locomotive propelling its train over the River Swale Bridge towards Boroughbridge, shortly before withdrawal of the passenger service in September 1950.
(MR 434703)
(Geoff Hockliffe)

The River Swale bridge photographed in 1989. The angle of the stonework in the barrel of the arch shows that the bridge is skew to the river.
(author)

Between Pilmoor and Knaresborough there were four level crossings. Pilmoor has already been described. The other three were between Brafferton and Boroughbridge: Wath Lane, Humberton and Myton Road.

Wath Lane crossing was the first, 1¼ mile from Brafferton. Wath Lane itself is a track that once formed the direct route from Helperby and Brafferton to Boroughbridge. The gatehouse was originally known as Brafferton Gate; it was on the left of the line as one travelled towards Boroughbridge.

Humberton (with pronunciation that stresses the second syllable) crossing was a quarter of a mile beyond Wath Lane on a track to Humberton Farm. The house was on the right of the line.

Finally, Myton Road crossing was ¾ mile beyond Humberton on Ellenthorpe Lane, which led to Ellenthorpe Hall Lodge and Clot House Farm, to the River Swale and over a bridge to Myton-on-Swale. Here too the house was on the right of the line.

Myton Road crossing was the scene of a minor accident on July 10th 1916. A special train consisting of a stores van ran through the gates, breaking them. The driver was blamed as, despite the fact that the gatewoman should have opened the gates, he had a clear view and should have stopped. This accident revealed that the North Eastern Railway had breached a section of the Railway Clauses Consolidation Act 1845, which required level crossing gates to be closed across the road, and therefore open to the railway, at all times when the railway was open for traffic. In other words the *normal* position of such gates was across the road. Road users were therefore expected to ask for the gates to be opened, except at night when they were left open to the road.

The buildings at the four crossings – Pilmoor, Wath Lane, Humberton and Myton Road – were of identical design. Each contained two semi-detached residences with five rooms apiece. The buildings, all of which remain to this day albeit some with the two residences knocked into one, are plain. The only architectural conceit is a blind window at each end of the upper floor. At the rear there is a single-storey extension. The roofs are of slate.

The residence nearest to the crossing was occupied by a railway employee whose wife took on the role of gatekeeper. The second residence was usually occupied by another employee but it was not uncommon for it to be let to a local farm worker. The gatehouse was rent-free; in effect the wife worked for the equivalent of the rent. Latterly rent was paid for the house and the wife received a wage, albeit a very low one.

In performing the gate duties husband and wife invariably formed a team. The wife was in charge full time when the husband was at his normal railway employment. At other times, bearing in mind that when the line was open someone always had to be in attendance, the husband and wife arranged things between them. On relatively quiet lines such as the Boroughbridge branch the duties of the crossing keeper were not onerous but it did mean that the husband or the wife was tied to the home at all times when the line was open for traffic. The only exception to this rule was when they were officially replaced by a 'relief crossing keeper'.

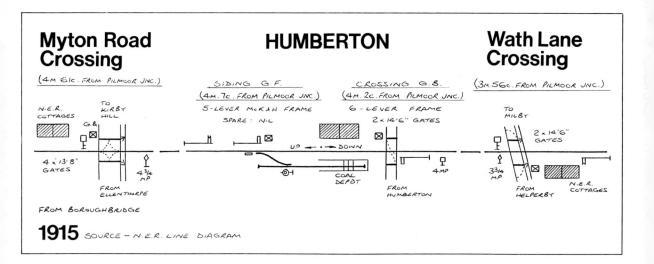

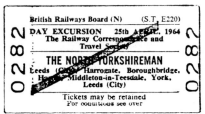

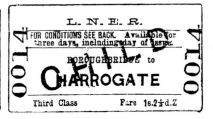

The ticket used by the author on the last passenger train to Boroughbridge together with two older examples from the collection of Geoffrey Lewthwaite.

Maurice Young with daughter standing outside his home, Humberton gatehouse, during the 1940s.
(MR 418691)
(Maurice Young)

The approach of a train was marked by the exchange of bell signals between Boroughbridge and Brafferton stations. 'Repeater' bells in the crossing keepers' houses also rang in sympathy, thus warning of the approach of a train. Mrs Evelyn Wedgwood was crossing keeper at Wath Lane for two years from 1937 to 1939. Her late husband, George Wedgwood, was a porter signalman at Brafferton station. She describes the daily life at the gates:

As gatekeeper I was paid, which was useful extra money. The bells were inside the house just above the front door. They gave a good ring, which startled me sometimes. I knew from the timetable when the passenger trains were coming but not the goods trains. There were no trains on Sundays apart from an occasional excursion. There were extra trains at other times and it wasn't so good if these trains came late at night because we used to have to sit up for them. There weren't many of them though.

There was a cabin next to the crossing on the opposite side of the road which contained the levers that I had to operate. If the gates were open to the road first you pulled one lever to unlock them. Then you went out and pushed the gates across the road. You went back into the cabin and locked the gates again with the same lever. Then you pulled another lever to pull the signal board off to let the train through. This board was quite a way down the line and there was one on each side of the crossing. (Author's note: these boards are described in section 11.)

When we were away we locked the house. Someone relieved me and had to stay in the cabin. There were no bells in the cabin but there was the telephone; however the relief crossing keeper could hear the bells from the house quite easily.

Maurice and Doris Young were married in 1944 and lived at Humberton for their first seven years. Mrs Young was the crossing keeper at Humberton for two of those years.

Joe Tuley was the ganger on the line during the War. Mrs Tuley was the gatekeeper and they had been there doing the gates for many years. Mr and Mrs Tuley retired but it was decided that they should stay in the gatekeeper's house. We took over the gates but, rather than move, the railway moved the bells into our house.

There was no running water in that house, but a pump in the wash-house outside. It was the same pump for both houses, with a handle and a spout on each side of the dividing fence. There was a wooden bung which you put in the spout on your side so that the other side could draw water. The water tended to come out of the lowest spout. If we forgot to put the bung in on our side and the other side started to pump, we would get most of the water and he might only get a trickle! It was good water and never did us any harm. There was no electricity and we had brass paraffin lamps with mantles. These were always very delicate things, but the lamps were very good.

During the War we used to get coal from the locomotive drivers. We always had about 30-40 hens and in exchange we gave them eggs. We had pigs which we killed for the bacon. You were allowed to kill a pig but accidentally two might get killed! We hung them up in a bedroom covered all over with muslin to keep the flies off. The meat would be carried away in suitcases and we could get more for the ham than the pigs were worth. There was a lot of that done. Doris would say 'What would you fancy for your supper?' and I would say 'We'll cut a piece off the shoulder and have a fry-up.'

Mrs Doris Bassitt and her late husband Arthur lived at Wath Lane for four years from 1954, after the passenger service on the branch had ceased and the level crossings had become unattended:

We had lived at Pilmoor where Arthur was signalman, but later he was on a summer relief job at Alne. We left Pilmoor to go to Wath Lane because we knew we could get electricity in there, although we had to put it in ourselves. The house had a big living room, a little scullery and a huge square pantry with a stone slab floor. In the scullery there was a sink and a tap for the water. We had only cold water, from a tap in the kitchen. The water was very hard and you couldn't get a lather with it. There were two huge rain water tubs in the wash-house and we used that for washing. There was an open yard with the wash-house, and a toilet, with the coal house at the end. We had two big bedrooms, one over the living room and one over the scullery. It was a nice house, because it got the sun.

Life for the families living at the crossings was not easy, not the least because for most of the day the husband or the wife had to be present to work the gates. Nevertheless former residents look back on those days with affection. Mrs

Wedgwood remembers that a gamekeeper used to call. Many a time she opened the crossing cabin to find a couple of rabbits or some pigeons on the seat. She and Mrs Pratt, wife of the Brafferton station master, exchanged visits, with one walking the 1¼ mile along the line to the other, usually with a young child in tow.

Humberton siding, looking towards Brafferton, in October 1964. *(John Mallon)*

At Humberton crossing there was a 48-yard-long siding with a two-cell coal depot at the end. Wagons were shunted into the siding as trains were travelling towards Boroughbridge although occasionally a train coming from Boroughbridge might have a wagon on the front, which was pushed straight into the siding.

The siding was used by the surrounding farms, principally Burton Grange and Humberton. Seasonal products such as sugar beet and potatoes were despatched from the siding, even hay. Goods received there included seed potatoes, fertilisers and, in the age of steam-powered farm machinery, coal. Wagons of Irish cattle were occasionally received.

Richard Wilkinson had Burton Grange farm from 1939:

We despatched sugar beet from the siding, which we took there with horses and carts. It was slavery: you had to load the railway truck by throwing everything up and over the truck side. At Boroughbridge on the other hand there was a proper loading dock; the top of the truck side was level with the top of the loading dock, and loading sugar beet, or potatoes or whatever it was, was easy. But I couldn't use Boroughbridge until I had a tractor with rubber tyres, which happened a year or so into the War. We then stopped taking stuff to Humberton siding. It was a lot easier with a rubber-tyred tractor and a biggish trailer to take it to Boroughbridge where you could chuck stuff down into the rail truck.

We didn't use the coal depot in Humberton siding when I came but I know that back in the earlier days they definitely brought threshing machine coal into that siding, and domestic coal too. The farmers would get together and they would buy a truck of coal, which they would split between them.

David Sowray and his family farmed at Humberton and remembers that the siding remained in use until about 1950:

We despatched sugar beet from there but we used to

receive sugar beet pulp too, for cattle feed. You sold the sugar beet to the factory and you got an allocation of pulp back. From memory you got a hundredweight and a half of pulp for every ton of beet you sent in. Pressed pulp had had the water pressed out of it and it used to come in rail trucks to the siding. It had a crust on it about a foot thick that formed a seal and it got quite warm. Unloading it was quite a nice job on a frosty morning. We received dried pulp too but usually by road. Occasionally there would be some surplus pulp, which we could buy but we had to take it in by rail.

We didn't receive livestock at Humberton siding, but I remember once getting a load of lambs there. They were for John Ramsden's at Myton. My father had been with him to Scotland to buy them. The lambs were coming down to Brafferton by train and they had to be walked to Myton. They were late coming and it was going to be too dark to walk them from Brafferton station. They got the train stopped at Humberton crossing. They put some doors down and ran them off onto the top of the siding, which was raised up at that point for the coal depot underneath. Then they ran them out into our field overnight, and walked them back across Myton Pastures the next day.

To make the coal depot high enough to permit a vehicle to be placed underneath, the siding was on a gradient. Not infrequently the users had to release the brakes of a wagon and let it run down to the very short level stretch at the beginning of the siding, taking care that it did not run away through the trap points and off the line. A sprag, left lying on the ground in the siding, could be place in the spokes of a wheel. David Sowray recalls that "on odd occasions a wagon got away and came off the line. We had to hang a tractor on it and pull it back on again."

The siding gradually fell out of use, although during the last years an occasional wagon was placed there.

5 Boroughbridge

Boroughbridge had two stations. The first station, for both passenger and goods, was opened on June 17th 1847. The passenger traffic was transferred to a second station on the opening of the line from Boroughbridge to Knaresborough on April 1st 1875. The first station remained open for goods throughout from 1847 until 1964.

The 1847 station consisted of two passenger platforms with station offices and waiting rooms, a large goods warehouse, coal depot, a lime shed at the end of the coal depot and a locomotive shed. According to the report of the Inspector for the Commissioners of Railways originally there was a turntable but there is no record of this on contemporary maps.

The accompanying plan, reproduced from an 1865 map, and photographs taken in more recent years give a good idea of how the original 1847 station appeared. The single-storey station building was 82 ft long, 23 ft deep. A wing at each end projected back into the station yard; a portico covered the area between the projecting wings. The two wings contained the ladies' waiting room and toilet and the general waiting room respectively. In the central section there was a gentlemen's waiting room, booking hall and office and combined porters' and lamp room. The station urinals, privies and coal house were between the station building and the station master's house. The latter has two floors; it is brick-built but with the quoins and the window and front door surrounds in stone. It has a shallow slate roof. A bedroom was added in 1891 and there was a further extension in 1894.

Water for the locomotive shed and a water column at the end of the 1847 passenger platforms came from Milby Cut. Later there was an additional water column near the 1875 passenger station and both remained in use until the railway was closed in 1964. In 1898 the NER built a new pump house on the boundary of the strip of land that led down to the Cut. The building measured 22ft 6in x 18ft 6in and was some 15ft high internally. The steam pumping engine occupied one side of the floor area and its chimney protruded through the roof. In 1905 a connection from this water supply was made to a self-filling drinking trough in a field belonging to Henry Brand, a Milby farmer, immediately to the north of the 1875 passenger station. In 1910 another connection was made to the adjacent Boroughbridge Farmers' Auction Mart.

In 1913 a recommendation that the steam pump be replaced by a hydraulic ram was agreed. Hydraulic rams can work for very long periods completely unattended. They are situated where water has to be brought a long distance from the source and where large volumes are needed, for example at railway stations. Moreover, after the initial costs of installation, the running costs are negligible.

Water from a stream or canal above the ram pours at speed down the supply pipe, forcing clacker valves to open. The water is impelled into an air vessel where it meets a cushion of air. Pressure very quickly builds up in the air vessel forcing the water back again to other clacker valves but, because of the great pressures involved, a small amount, perhaps a cupful only, is directed up a narrow pipe from the air vessel. A non-return valve prevents the water returning to the ram. The cycle repeats itself and, although only a small amount of water is pumped each time, the sequence continues 24 hours a day, 365 days a year. The typical noise of a ram pump is a thump-thump-thump that can be heard (and felt) over long distances.

The only time a ram will stop is if debris gets under a clacker valve and prevents it from closing, if a clack wears out, if the ram chamber is flooded or during a prolonged and deep frost. A filter over the mouth of the feeder prevents debris from getting in.

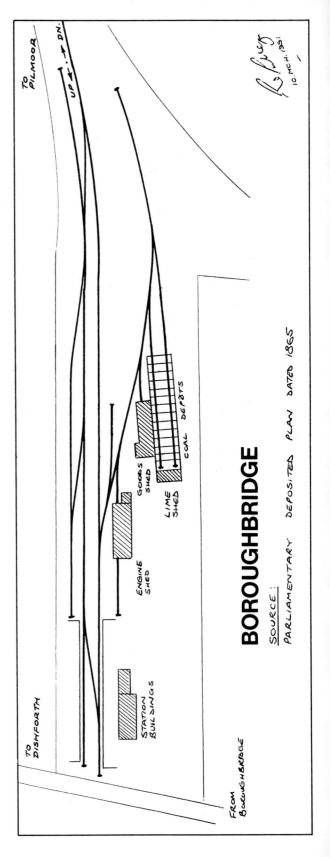

BOROUGHBRIDGE

SOURCE:
PARLIAMENTARY DEPOSITED PLAN DATED 1865

The 1847 Boroughbridge passenger station, with the station master's house on the left, in April 1964. (MR 397673)
(author)

Boroughbridge station master's house during the 1950s. Note the cattle wagons on the right, in the former passenger platform, later cattle dock.
(courtesy of Mary Watson)

Boroughbridge station master's house in 1990. *(author)*

The 1847 Boroughbridge passenger station, station master's house on the left, on April 30th 1949.
(© John Armstrong/courtesy of the John Armstrong Trustees)

Boroughbridge goods station on April 30th, 1949: left, the original locomotive shed, converted in 1896 into a goods warehouse; centre, the main goods warehouse. The 1847 passenger station is beyond the water crane on the right. *(© John Armstrong/courtesy of the John Armstrong Trustees)*

The Boroughbridge hydraulic ram was built by Blakes of Accrington and was a big one. It was situated on the island between the River Ure and Milby Cut. It was buried in a chamber some 12 feet square. The height of the Cut above the ram was 12 to 13 feet and the water was fed from the Cut by a pipe of about six inches diameter. The surplus water from the ram ran away to the River Ure. The pumped water travelled to large tanks adjacent to the 1875 station, serving the water columns at the passenger station and goods yard. In a twelve-year period it required attention only three times, because of debris under the clack. To prevent silt backing up when the River Ure was in flood the permanent way men occasionally cleaned the ram chamber out.

For the 1875 Boroughbridge to Knaresborough extension to have commenced from the end of the existing line from Pilmoor would have made it too low in relation to the River Ure; the gradient required to bridge the river with adequate clearance would have been too steep. The extension therefore commenced a quarter of a mile back from the end of the 1847 line.

A new passenger station was necessary and was built adjacent to the road from Boroughbridge to Kirby Hill and the north (until 1962 the A1). It had a platform on each side of a passing loop, the only one between Pilmoor and Knaresborough and which fell out of use before even the end of the 19th century. The single-storey station building was on the southbound platform. It was 102ft 3in long, with a 67ft 3in central section flanked by a wing at each end. Each wing projected 10ft 10½in at the front and by 10ft at the back. The central section was 17ft 7½in deep. There were shallow pitched roofs and a glass verandah on the platform between the wings.

The northern wing, nearest Pilmoor, contained a staff room, the ladies' waiting room and toilet, a coal house and lamp room. The central section had a spacious station master's office, a gentlemen's first class waiting room and general waiting room, both the latter with toilets. Between the central section and the southern wing a passage led through from the station yard to the platform. This passage also formed the booking hall, with the booking office itself in the southern wing. A small area of the booking office was a parcels office, entered from the platform. The rear part of the southern wing contained the urinals. On the northbound platform there was a small building, later used for storing coal and sand.

The signalbox was a low, greenhouse-like building at the Knaresborough end of the southbound platform. In 1892 it had twelve working levers and three spare, later altered to fourteen working levers and one spare, but these were all dispensed with in 1936 (see Section 11).

In 1877 the buildings of the 1847 passenger station were converted into two homes. Each had a living room, three bedrooms, scullery, pantry, coal house and privy, the last accessible only from outside on the old station platform. The station master continued living in the original station master's house, which remains at the time of writing. Walter Watson became station master at Boroughbridge in 1954, four years after the end of the passenger service. His widow, Mrs Mary Watson, has clear recollections of what she found when she and her husband first inspected the house:

When we first went to view the station house, before Walter applied for the job, I had such a shock as we walked into the kitchen. The place was an absolute shambles. From the ceiling great long strings of emulsion paint were hanging down. In the hall there was one pattern of wallpaper going up halfway and another above that. While we were there looking it over another station master's wife was doing the same and I could hear her talking to her husband: 'I won't have this and you needn't put your name down for this station.' She was chuntering away but all you needed was new wallpaper and new paint and it was a beautiful place. And it didn't cost us anything for the paper, because the railway paid the first 2s 6d for the paper and you paid anything over that. You could get papers at 6d a roll in those days.

I was right and it was a lovely house. As you went in through the front door there was a big entrance hall on the right. There were only three rooms downstairs but they were very big. To the right there was the sitting room. Straight ahead there was the kitchen and the dining room. A wide staircase led up onto a landing and then on up to the next landing. Upstairs there were four bedrooms and a bathroom. Our bedroom overlooked the Cut. It had windows on three sides. It had a fireplace with a gas fire but we never used it. We had running water and a toilet upstairs and in the yard downstairs. We had gas lighting.

There was a big yard between the cottages (the old 1847 station buildings) and the station house. There was a huge garden opposite the house. It had an orchard, with every tree you could imagine. There had been a tennis court at one time, and a greenhouse too. It was a nice garden but it had been neglected, because the man before us had had no family and hadn't bothered with the garden.

From our bedroom window we faced straight east. One morning I experienced something that has lived with me ever since. It was summer and the curtains were drawn back. There was an eerie feeling and I wondered what it was. It was the sun rising and the most glorious scene I've ever seen. Everything was grey: the grass and the trees silhouetted against the sky. Then the greyness and the darkness gradually moved away as the fingers of the dawn came creeping up. Then one bird broke the silence and the dawn chorus started. I've never seen a dawn like it since. It reminded me of when I lived on a farm and I was the dairy maid. My sister and I used to get up at 4 am to make the butter. One very, very hot summer, when we'd made the butter we left it in the big barrel, standing in cold water. We used to lean over the stackyard gate and watch the sun rise.

In its heyday Boroughbridge employed a large number of staff. In the mid-1920s there were three clerks in the goods office, one of whom was the chief clerk, and in the yard there was a yard foreman and two or three goods porters. There were two more clerks up at the passenger station and two porter signalmen. In 1960, there were two clerks and two porters but by that time the station dealt exclusively with goods traffic.

As can be seen from Appendix A the passenger traffic at Boroughbridge was greater than from the other stations: 73 per day in 1895. Nevertheless the decline was relatively more severe than at the other stations, with a daily average of 15 in 1940.

As well as their human cargo the passenger trains also carried parcels and even living produce. Bill Lake, one time station master at Pilmoor, recalls goats from a Boroughbridge breeder, Miss Mostyn Owen, going on the train to Pilmoor for connection with a main line train. Strangely, there were passenger parcels even after the passenger service ceased.

For many years Miss Betsy Mudd of Aldborough Dairy had customers all over the country for her cheeses. Miss Mudd's cheeses were highly regarded and regularly won prizes at the London Dairy Show, to which they were sent by rail. Towards Christmas Dick Watson, clerk in the late 1950s (no relation to Watler Watson), handled twenty or thirty cartons of cheese a day from Miss Mudd's Dairy. "They would always come as full, round cheeses in hessian coverings, big and hard. The cartons were rather flimsy and were secured with binder twine. There were very large despatches

The fine timber roof of the Boroughbridge goods warehouse, photographed in 1990. *(author)*

and they would go on the pickup to Knaresborough every morning and be transferred to the passenger trains there." As well as sending milk to the Aldborough Dairy, however, local farmers loaded churns on the first morning passenger train to Harrogate, whence it went to Hindle's Dairy, later Craven Dairy, in Leeds, and doubtless to other dairies.

At the appropriate time of the year a local plant nursery would despatch 30 or 40 cartons of chrysanthemums and dahlias for distribution nationally.

As with many country stations goods traffic at Boroughbridge was predominant. As remarked above and elsewhere, the goods station remained in the same location throughout the life of the branch. However, as can be seen from the accompanying maps, the layout of the goods yard was quite different when it was first opened from what it later became.

On entering the yard from the road from Boroughbridge to Dishforth the buildings of the original 1847 passenger station were on the left, with the station master's house at the far end. On the right there was the station master's 100-yard-long garden, referred to earlier by Mrs Watson.

Beyond the station house, and still with the garden on the right, there stood the goods warehouse, with its office and weighbridge on the nearmost corner. The warehouse measured 100ft 2in in length, 42ft 10½in wide and 22ft high. There were two doors at each end, one for the rail track that ran through the building and the other for the road delivery vehicles. Inside there were two one-ton derricks, with the top pivot of each fixed to the roof beams and the bottom to the raised timber deck. At one end there was a porters' room, with a cooking stove and small muniment room.

The goods office was at the front adjacent to the weighbridge and measured 21ft 8in long, 11ft 5in wide. There were two rooms for the clerks one of which contained the weigh scale. The office desks were high sloping ones, typical of those to be seen in thousands of railway offices, at which the clerks sat on tall stools. However for most of the time they were on their feet, attending to the weighbridge or going down the yard to attend to this, that or the other. The office lighting was by gas. In the common memory, the gas

lights hissed and blowed, shedding a golden light across the office.

The coal depot was beyond the warehouse. There were fourteen cells and, as the depot itself had a double track, 28 wagons could be accommodated. The coal business at Boroughbridge was a big one, with several coal merchants competing with each other and with the station master. However, some of the coal was brought in by road by the local merchants and the depot was merely a convenient place to store it.

Another building loomed up behind the coal depot. This was the locomotive shed that was a part of the 1847 station. In 1896 it was made redundant and was converted into a second goods warehouse. The building was 87ft 2in long, 27ft wide and 24ft to the apex of the roof. Vents to let locomotive smoke escape added another four feet to the height. It was used mainly for handling and storing bulk commodities. In 1926 this warehouse was let to William Maltby, grocer and corn merchant, at a rent of £30 per annum. Later it was used by Yorkshire Farmers, and later still by Boots for the distribution of chemicals and fertilisers.

Passing the coal depot on the left there was a siding on the right. This was the station's most versatile siding, being 150 yards long and the site of the loading dock, five-ton crane, and the facilities that were later added for the Anglo-American Oil Co. and Blundy Clark. Adjacent to this long siding there was the strip of land that led down to the bank of Milby Cut. The early steam pumping engine for the station's water supply was here. Also near here there were allotment gardens used by Arthur Clayton, chief clerk, and Bob Pinkney, motor driver, among others.

On the side of the main station buildings away from the yard entrance there were the two tracks of the original passenger station, used later for general wagon storage but, more importantly, as the livestock loading dock. The many sidings converged some 350 yards from the yard entrance, making the whole place large, spacious and easily worked by goods trains.

Until 1892 rail access to the goods yard was controlled by Boroughbridge Goods Junction signalbox, opened with the extension to Knaresborough in 1875. Little is known about this signalbox, other than its location. It controlled one end of the Boroughbridge passing loop on the through line from Pilmoor to Knaresborough and the junction into the goods yard. On the evidence of the report of a Board of Trade Inspector in 1875 there were at least eleven levers.

The Goods Junction signalbox was closed in 1892 and most of its functions were transferred to the remaining signalbox at the 1875 passenger station. Looking from the station towards Pilmoor the line appeared double. The left track was the single line to Pilmoor. The right track was the goods line and eventually ended as a long shunting neck, known as Milby siding. Nearly half a mile from the passenger station, a pair of hand-worked points controlled the junction down into the goods yard.

The goods traffic was handled by the goods porters and porter signalmen. Eric Jackson, motor delivery driver, remembers that:

One porter was George Johnson. We always called him 'Bandy' Johnson, I don't know why. Then there was Ted Wymer and Harry Schofield as well, goods porters. One of them was the senior porter but they used to work together. There was also a lad porter, who ticketed wagons. There was a shunter in the yard but Ted Wymer did most of the shunting. The yard was a big one and it took quite a lot to shunt it.

Up at the passenger station there was Tommy Greenfield and Harold Hunt, porter signalmen. They worked at the passenger station but when they were both on duty in the middle of the day one of them was in the yard helping to load the full loads. Whoever was on the late turn had to come down to the yard after the last passenger train.

Joyce Coates, whose father Bob Pinkney was another of Boroughbridge's motor delivery drivers, remembers how 'Bandy' Johnson probably acquired his nickname:

Eric Jackson had a particular rope that he fastened the sheet over his loads down with and he often got Dad to give him a hand to pull it tight with some sort of instrument. One day between them they broke the rope. Eric was very upset because it was a very particular rope. My Dad said "Give it to Bandy". Bandy spliced the rope and it was as good as new. Evidently he had had a job working with ropes before coming to Boroughbridge as porter. We always assumed that Bandy was his name because he was bandy-legged. Bands are what farmers call ropes and string, and it must have been because of his skill with ropes that he got the name.

Dick Watson, at Boroughbridge in the late 1950s, recalls that:

The station master had his coal sale but there were three or four other coal merchants: George Wright, Thompsons, Sadlers and Atkinsons, some of whom only rented the space. They were big, independent businesses. The station master's sale was as big as theirs but most of his sales were large bulk deliveries to farmers who would come and collect on a trailer, a minimum of a ton at a time.

There was one incident when the station master, Mr Watson, went to Brafferton and I manned the office. The porters were busy doing something else in the yard and he told me that Sadlers would be coming for a load of coke and the bottom door of their hopper wagon up on the depot had to be opened for them. When they arrived I had to make sure that the coal was duly discharged from the railway hopper wagon up above into the trailer underneath. When Sadlers arrived I went along, but unfortunately I didn't properly gauge the opening of the bottom door on the hopper wagon. So, instead of allowing about five tons, about 20

tons descended and it totally buried this trailer underneath. The guy spent the rest of the day digging himself out. Mr Watson wasn't pleased and I'd been proved less than capable at managing the coal business!

Down at the bottom of the goods yard there was a potato dock which was built up on sleepers so that carts could back up and tip everything straight into the wagons. We had to throw purple dye on them to signify that they had been sold to the Potato Marketing Board who were aranging disposal. There was a glut whilst I was there and we dealt with hundreds of wagons of potatoes, most of which were exported via Goole. We had a coal fire in the office and for a couple of months during the potato harvesting season we had jacket potatoes continuously!

A lot of sugar beet also went away, largely to the York sugar beet factory. When that was congested it would be directed either to Selby or to Netherfield and Colwick. But sacks, and their contents, were important. As elsewhere the farmers rented their sacks from the railway. The sacks themselves were very durable, strong ones. Even in the late 1950s, not long before the railway sack business was sold, many of the sacks still had the letters 'L.N.E.R.' stencilled on them.

The railway charged for the sacks in two ways: for the actual hire of the sacks and demurrage for the length of time that they were retained by the hirer. For clerk Dick Watson the sack business held fewer terrors than for many of his colleagues at other stations:

You were forever recording the movement of sacks. There were movements of sacks when you weren't always aware of the full details and they were not properly recorded. A farmer might hire some sacks and they might disappear because he had passed them on without telling us. You might find that out only when someone else told you that they had been returned. Of course if you levied all the charges against the hiring farmer up to the time when the sacks were eventually returned by the, say, third or fourth party, he would squeal and you would find out that he had transferred them on a certain date. It was like a big jigsaw working out where sacks had gone and who was responsible for the charges.

As befits the large town that it served Boroughbridge station also handled a multitude of different goods traffics. There was a store for Silcocks animal feeding stuffs. Wagons would arrive on most days and the bags were unloaded into the store, a pre-fabricated concrete shed near the coal depot line. The local Silcocks salesman, Angus Tear, seemed to the staff of the late 1950s to have won all the farmers over to his company.

At this time one of the main forwarders from Boroughbridge was the firm of Titherley's. They dealt in washed rags, sponge cloths and the like for industry, for general cleaning purposes. They came in to Titherley's by road, were washed and turned into clean dusters for despatch all over the country in large cardboard boxes. It was not unusual for there to be three or four wagons of Titherley's cloths in a day.

In 1904 the Anglo-American Oil Co. Ltd. signed a contract with the NER to lease 258 square yards of land at the bottom of the goods yard to house two petrol tanks, an office and pump house. The oil company erected a standpipe at the end of the siding with a connection to the tanks. The agreement provided for the possibility that the oil company might want to make its own new siding, but this was never done.

In the early days of George Wright a lot of timber went through the station:

In 1919 the Ouseburn Estate, which belonged to Lord

Knaresborough, was sold. A gang of farmers and developers from Thirsk bought it. They used to call them the Forty Thieves, because they stripped the estate of all the fellable timber. Greens of Silsden bought it and they sent it through Boroughbridge station. At the station there was a special gang that came out from Harrogate to load the timber onto wagons.

The timber came to the station on horse-drawn wood carts with very broad wheels. The streets of Boroughbridge were stone and earth in those days and not made for heavy loads. The main York road was ankle deep in puddles and ruts. This went on for three or four years while the trees were cut down. The timber was loaded in the long siding at the bottom of the yard, nearest to the canal, where there was a crane.

In the 1920s another traffic was important. In 1860 the company of Sanders and Smith had been sold a piece of land near the River Ure for a malt kiln. Raw barley was taken in from the farmers to the maltings and was processed into what goes to make ale. The offal from the barley went to make cattle feed, which was despatched by rail. The malt was used by the nearby brewery. At one side of the main line towards Knaresborough there was a coal shute down into the brewery yard, a very unusual arrangement in that a wagon would have to be discharged while it stood on the main line. There are no memories of the use of this shute.

As remarked earlier, the railway property at Borough-bridge included a piece of land from the goods yard down to Milby Cut. Adjacent to this the company Blundy Clark Ltd. brought sand and gravel from up the River Ure to be screened and despatched by rail. In 1934 Blundy Clark erected an overhead gantry from the Cut to convey gravel to the goods yard. The gantry was a local landmark for more than 30 years. In the memories of the staff of the goods station little was despatched by rail. Some, however, did go by rail to the railway's Leeman Road, York, concrete depot.

Perhaps the business that has left the strongest impression on the former staff of Boroughbridge is cattle. Monday was market day. Before Frank Hick joined the railway in 1922 he had worked at Ramsden's farm at Myton and he himself used to drive all kinds of livestock the five miles to Boroughbridge market, see them sold and walk back in the evening. He started working at Boroughbridge station in 1924:

When I came to work at Boroughbridge station we used to send out up to 80 or 100 wagons of livestock, two fully loaded trains every Monday. These trains went out via Starbeck where they were broken up and despatched to wherever they were destined. Most of it went to the West Riding: Leeds, Bradford, Keighley, Halifax, but we got the odd cattle train to York or to Newcastle. I don't remember anything very much coming in, although there was the odd wagon of cattle or sheep. The farmers would go up to Scotland and buy, say, sheep and they would be despatched by rail and arrive at Boroughbridge, or at Brafferton, a few days later.

The livestock all had to be invoiced, with the correct number of animals recorded. I remember making a real faux pas with this. We used to send cattle to Bradford. We also used to send cattle to Keighley but the trouble was that there was a man named Keighley at Bradford. So one day, inevitably, Mr Keighley's traffic was sent to Keighley instead of Bradford. We did get into trouble over that but that was the sort of thing that happened.

On Monday mornings the trains of empty cattle wagons were brought in from Starbeck and shunted into Milby siding, the shunting neck for the line down into the goods yard.

The cattle market itself, the Boroughbridge Farmers' Auction Mart referred to earlier, was very close to the station; indeed the NER leased land to the mart in 1920 to enable it to expand. Most of the animals were sent away by rail and were driven on the hoof to the cattle dock at the 1847 station, the former passenger platform furthest from the house. The livestock went out in mid afternoon, sometimes in two trains. During the War market day was changed to a Tuesday because there were too many Monday market days generally and there were not enough cattle wagons to cater for them all.

By the late 1950s the cattle business, as far as the railway was concerned, had virtually ceased. On market day fewer than a dozen wagons went out. The empty wagons had been delivered by the pickup at the end of the preceding week but a locomotive came from Starbeck or York to take the loaded wagons away after the market.

At the end of its life Boroughbridge goods station was very quiet. Its staff consisted only of Walter Watson, station master, Sylvia Mann (née Horner), clerk, Harold Hunt, goods porter, Bob Pinkney, motor driver. It was finally closed on October 2nd 1964.

30

The 1875 Boroughbridge passenger station in the 1930s, looking south west. A horse box is occupying the former passing loop. (MR 394672) (©Douglas Thompson)

Push and pull train at Boroughbridge, date unknown but probably during the 1940s.
(courtesy of Ken Taylor)

Opposite A long standing feature of the passenger timetable was the running of trains on certain days of the week only. This alternate Mondays Harrogate to Boroughbridge return working ran throughout most of the 1920s in connection with the cattle market. At one stage it was withdrawn but then reinstated.
(David Beeken collection)

Richard Cawood, Boroughbridge station master from 1922 to 1933.
(courtesy of Philip Cawood)

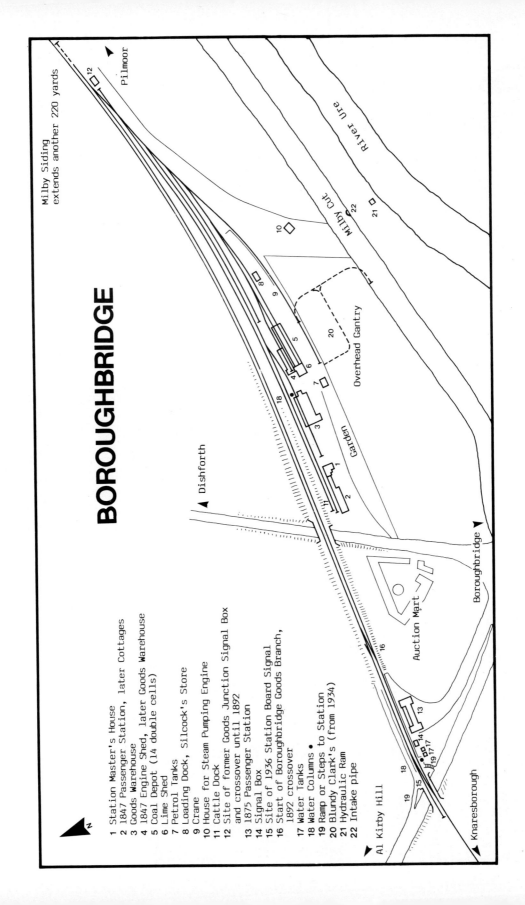

BOROUGHBRIDGE

Milby Siding
extends another 220 yards

Pilmoor

River Ure

Milby Cut

Overhead Gantry

Dishforth

Garden

Auction Mart

Boroughbridge

A1 Kirby Hill

Knaresborough

1 Station Master's House
2 1847 Passenger Station, later Cottages
3 Goods Warehouse
4 1847 Engine Shed, later Goods Warehouse
5 Coal Depot (14 double cells)
6 Lime Shed
7 Petrol Tanks
8 Loading Dock, Silcock's Store
9 Crane
10 House for Steam Pumping Engine
11 Cattle Dock
12 Site of former Goods Junction Signal Box
   and crossover until 1892
13 1875 Passenger Station
14 Signal Box
15 Site of 1936 Station Board Signal
16 Start of Boroughbridge Goods Branch,
   1892 crossover
17 Water Tanks
18 Water Columns
19 Ramp or Steps to Station
20 Blundy Clark's (from 1934)
21 Hydraulic Ram
22 Intake pipe

An aerial view of the railway at Boroughbridge, June 3rd 1951, with the River Nidd bridge left, the 1847 passenger station left of centre and the 1847 station centre. Milby Cut is close to the railway, with the River Nidd beyond it.

(© Crown copyright/MOD, reproduced with the permission of HMSO)

Boroughbridge passenger station May 11th 1958, looking south east with the malt kiln in the background, signalbox centre.
(Jim Sedgwick)

The southern end of Boroughbridge passenger station, with the twin water tanks filled by the hydraulic ram pump, signalbox, water crane and, on the right, the Station Board, part of the 1936 signalling scheme.
(J.W. Hague courtesy of David Beeken)

6 River Ure Bridge and Roecliffe Siding

River Ure Bridge

A quarter of a mile beyond Boroughbridge passenger station the railway crossed the River Ure by a two-span girder bridge. The four wrought iron main girders – two per span – were of identical 125-foot length. River clearance was about eighteen feet.

There were six cast iron piers: two on each bank and two in the centre of the river. Although the bridge itself was straight the railway over it was curved. The rails were fixed on 12-inch-square longitudinal timbers. The outer rail of the curve was superelevated, which made life a little tricky for the augmented track maintenance gang when, as happened several times over the years, these timbers were renewed.

Finally, the line over the bridge was at a gradient of 1 in 218, descending towards Knaresborough, with the result that one end of the bridge was some ten inches higher than the other.

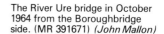

The River Ure bridge in October 1964 from the Boroughbridge side. (MR 391671) *(John Mallon)*

The last passenger train ever to use the branch heading back to Knaresborough over the River Ure bridge, April 25th 1964. *(author)*

Roecliffe Siding

As the time for the opening of the line from Boroughbridge to Knaresborough approached, the inhabitants of the nearby villages of Minskip and Roecliffe asked the NER for their own station. The NER refused the request but they were more amenable when, in June 1882, Mr Joseph William Green applied for a siding to serve his nearby brick and tileworks.

Bricks and tiles from Roecliffe were used in a wide area, although latterly it was found that the clay was more suited to the manufacture of tiles than of bricks. Subsequently the works concentrated on tiles for both roofs and land drainage. Although bricks ceased to be manufactured the works remained known as 'the brickworks'.

The brickworks were served by a small landing stage on the River Ure nearby, into which coal and sand came and from which bricks were despatched downstream to York and beyond. In the year 1881 the amount of brickworks traffic forwarded and received by rail was 2,548 tons (presumably being carted to and from Boroughbridge station), and that forwarded and received by water was 4,049 tons. When in June 1882 Mr Green applied for the siding he declared that he would work his traffic to it by means of a tramway from his works.

The siding agreement was signed on September 2nd 1882. It specified that it should be used for no other purpose than ''the reception of coal, coke and other materials as may be required to be consumed . . . for the purposes of carrying on his business as a manufacturer and for the forwarding of such bricks, tiles, pipes and other articles manufactured by said works''. The agreement was assigned to United Tile Manufacturers Ltd. (UTM) in October 1936.

The siding was 116 yards long and held up to twelve wagons. Its points faced in the direction of Knaresborough. At the buffer end there were two cells for coal to the brick kilns. Access was controlled by a covered ground frame, with six levers for the points into the siding and the signals on both sides, and one spare lever.

Memories of the rail traffic that came out of the Roecliffe siding are provided by Frank Hick, from his days as a clerk at Boroughbridge in the 1920s:

There was a lot of traffic from Green's brickyard. By and large they were good customers to the railway. Their bricks went around quite a large radius, mostly to Leeds but also to Lincolnshire, the rest of Yorkshire, Lancashire and Durham. Their chief clerk was called Sutcliffe; he really knew his business. He talked authoritatively to you and, if you questioned him on a particular requirement, you knew he was genuine. He was a very efficient man. But we always had a problem there with wagon supplies, obtaining the right kind of descriptions of the traffic that was in the wagons and getting the wagons collected by the pickup. Then we also had problems with breakages of tiles and slates, which we had difficulty in assessing and checking the evaluations of the losses that the firm claimed from the breakages.

Traffic from the brickyard declined during the 1940s. In August 1948 Mr H. Grant, Director and Secretary of UTM, wrote to BR to the effect that the Company had ''come to the decision that the siding is too distant from the works and that it cannot be used profitably by us''. The agreement was terminated from February 18th 1949.

The tramway originally intended to serve the siding was never built. However in 1899 Mr Green made a second application to the NER, for a subway under the railway to accommodate a tramway from a new clayfield to the main brickworks. This was granted on the basis that Mr Green would pay the cost of making the bridge and of its maintenance. This bridge, No. 12 from Pilmoor, is shown on later railway maps as Klondike Bridge.

The brickworks and the new clayfield were respectively east and west of the Boroughbridge branch railway. There were four kilns but in 1954 or 1955 a new brickworks, also west of the railway and containing three kilns, was opened. The old brickworks remained in use.

In the clayfield there was a layer of topsoil up to six feet deep. This was followd by no fewer than 24 feet of clay above a layer of water-filled gravel. Clay was excavated down to its maximum depth, subject only to leaving a narrow layer above the gravel in order to prevent flooding from below (not always successfully).

While the tramway was never directly involved with the Boroughbridge branch, it is worth relating its history. It was of two-foot gauge and originally a double line from the clayfield to the old brickworks, passing under the railway by the aforementioned subway. It was powered by an endless rope, which was crude but effective, and very dangerous. One disadvantage was that it could not go round corners; contemporary maps show sections of straight track connected with several distinct corners. 'Corner boys' were employed to assist the tubs round these corners.

After the endless rope was abandoned the tramway was singled. Three forms of traction were subsequently used. Battery trams were first, followed by electric locomotives. The 80-volt electric locomotives were by Brush Electrical Engineers, powered from a third rail. It is not known how many of these locomotives were used, but it will not have been more than two or three, and maybe was only one. Finally a diesel locomotive was acquired. This was a four-wheeled locomotive manufactured by F.C. Hibberd & Co. Ltd., numbered 2466. In 1946 a second diesel locomotive was bought, Ruston and Hornsby 237888.

There was a branch to a part of the works that made special types of tiles. Along this branch there was a shed for one of the diesel locomotives, made out of an old six-wheeled main line passenger coach. In the clayfield short branches were thrown out from the tramway, and small turntables gave access to all corners. The clay tubs were pushed about by hand.

A branch was laid to the new brickworks. It climbed some twelve feet up from the clayfield on a steep gradient. As a locomotive descended to the clayfield it sanded the rails in preparation for its return with three tubs of clay. The sand was dried in the nearby kilns. The gradient to the old works was somewhat easier, enabling between six and eight tubs to be hauled.

The length of the tramway varied as the new clayfield was gradually extended. At its peak it would have been no more than about half a mile in overall length, including the branches but excluding the short stretches in the clayfield. In 1959 there were eighteen four-wheeled wagons: twelve end-tippers, four side-tippers, two flat wagons.

George Pratt, who worked at the brickworks for very many years, is the best authority on its workings:

At the main line siding many a time there would be seven or eight wagons of tiles or pipes for a train to gather up. I've done the ticketing of them, all labelled 'shunt with care'. It held coal for the works too in coal cells at the far end of the siding. Nearly every day the train had to call. We once had an order for 25,000 tiles a week to Middlesbrough. Mr Albert Gough was the foreman, and he used to say 'If only we can keep these 25,000 tiles going out every week it'll keep us in a wage.'

The tramway was a double line with a separate line for the wagons going to the mill and for the empty wagons going back to be filled. It went through a cutting and under the railway girder bridge. There was just room under the railway bridge; we had to put thin three-inch sleepers for the rails in there because they wouldn't take the normal five-inch sleepers and let the tubs underneath the bridge.

The tubs were hauled by an endless rope, driven from the old yard with a big steam engine. The rope was up in the air on a big structure, although it used to run on rollers on the ground behind the tubs. But the rope couldn't go round corners and there were big wheels that put the rope to face straight down the next section of the track. They had corner boys, whose job was to get the tubs round these wheels. When I was 15 I got to be corner boy.

A truck was fixed onto the endless rope by a clip. The rope rested on the top of the truck; there were two gimbals at the back and this iron thing with a mouthpiece on it was slotted into the gimbals. You shut the jaws of the mouthpiece onto the rope. Then you had to cosh it with a stick, like a big heavy lump of wood with a hammer part to it. You used to have to strike it three or four times to get it to hold and pick it up. If you were too clever it would pick the truck off its wheels, and then you had a job! It was a marvellous thing but I always said that that endless rope was just like taking the devil by the tail. You could have your hand sliced off nearly, it got that bad.

At each end of the tramway the endless rope was lapped two or three times round a wheel. There was an iron bar over the line which we called the 'knock off'. It released the clip and the steel rope flew out of the mouthpiece. At the filling station in the clayfield you kept putting new lines in, extending them over this clay. You pushed your wagons around there by hand, and then back to the endless rope, hooked them on and they were away.

There was a wire at the side of the rope about as thick as your finger. If anything was going wrong and any tubs were off the line, you had to grab hold of this bell wire and run with your body at it. That used to blow a whistle, and it released the rope and stopped the job. That was for emergencies and there were a lot of them. If there was a big disaster, if you'd three or four tubs off, men out of the clay hole had to come

and reload them.

At any time there would be about 30 wagons in use, but some of them weren't fit to be. Some of them had lumps of flange out and sometimes the flange would hit the back of the rail and it was no wonder that it came off the line.

They were professionals who came to splice the endless rope together and it used to cost a big figure. But eventually, it was so expensive that it was given over, rather than buy another rope. Instead they got these battery trams. I thought I was in heaven when I was driving the tram. You plugged the battery in to charge while you had your dinner. Then you pulled it out when you came back again, and set off as hard as you could. They were flea-blown things, and by three o'clock in the afternoon we'd used all the power there was in them. Nobody ever told me about the acid for filling the batteries with.

After that we had proper electric power from an electrified rail at the side of the track. But no-one knew anything about electricity! The electric rail was steel; a lot of them were old rails from the track and they connected them up with copper wire at the joints. They even went as far as cutting a great lump out of that endless rope to gather the electricity out of. There were no insulators and they wasted no end of power. You could see it spitting out. This was a mistake but thank God it wasn't strong or half of us would have been killed. But as soon as we got that we went places. You could take three empties one way and three full'uns the other. But it was a mistake and nobody would admit it. It never had a chance. It could have pulled three times as much if it had been up out of the road with an overhead cable. It would have been a proper job then. The electric engines were in use when I went into the army during the War. It was diesel when I came back out.

The brickworks were closed in August 1963 and were sold and demolished in the following year. The site is now occupied by a small industrial estate.

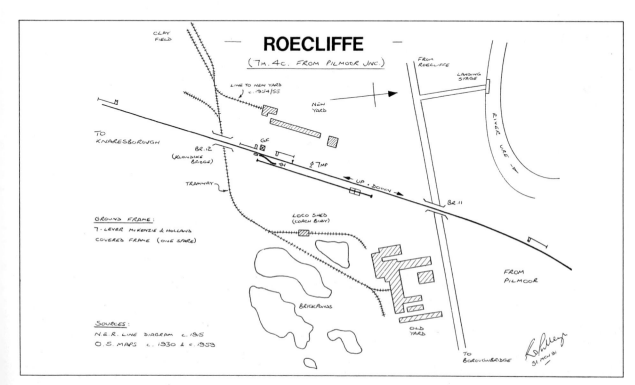

7 Copgrove

Copgrove is an example of a station whose name was not what one might have expected. The village of Staveley was less than half a mile from the station and was the obvious name to use, but there was the possibility of confusion with Staveley in Derbyshire. Copgrove is a little more than a mile beyond Staveley and the joint name 'Copgrove and Staveley' was adopted from its opening in 1875. For a short period there were references to 'Staveley and Copgrove' until November 1881 when the single name 'Copgrove' became permanent.

At the front of the station a long sweeping drive led uphill from the road between Staveley and Arkendale towards the station entrance. Here the station master had his garden, with a pig sty. Branching off this drive near its start another drive led past the goods weighbridge and the buffers for the station's main siding to the five-cell coal depot. Unlike the coal depots at Brafferton and Boroughbridge the one at Copgrove had only a single line. There was no crane nor goods warehouse.

The station building was a large one, with a ground floor similar in plan to the 1875 passenger station at Borough-bridge, built at the same time. There were two wings, one single-storey, the other double. The former contained the station offices; the latter was the residence of the station master. A long single-storey central section held a large waiting room. The area on the platform between the wings was covered by a glass verandah.

At the Pilmoor end of the station building there were various rooms and outhouses: gents toilets, a lamproom and a wash-house for the house. At the Knaresborough end there was a small signalbox that remained even after conventional signals were ablished in 1936. It had eleven working and no spare levers; measuring 12 feet by 10 feet, it was identical to that at Boroughbridge passenger station.

Copgrove station early in the 20th century, looking towards Knaresborough (top) with the station master and two sons, with his two-man staff. Some idea of the magnificence of the station garden can be seen in the lower photograph, looking towards Boroughbridge. (MR 367622)

In the house there were living room, dining room, kitchen and bathroom. The living room looked out onto the platform with the dining room at the back adjacent to the kitchen. Upstairs there were four bedrooms, one of which was in an ugly extension built in 1915 for station master Jack Skilbeck and his large family. This was faced in brick but was later rendered.

During the 1930s, when Copgrove no longer had its own station master, the house was divided into two flats. Even when the station master was restored the division remained. In the late 1940s the upstairs flat was occupied by Derrek and Alice Trinder, he being the station master, and the other by Clarrie and Mary Fawcett and his mother. Water was a common problem for it all had to be pumped into tanks, one for each home, with the pump itself in the lamproom. There was but one pump, with a valve to direct the water into the correct tank. In the wash-house each family had a tap from its own water tank. The families always rued the day when they inadvertently pumped the water into the wrong tank, or when they used the wrong water in the wash-house.

In 1877 the Great Ouseburn Union Rural Sanitary Authority reported very unfavourably on the hygenic standards at the station:

The cesspool in the yard adjoining the dwelling which drains into the first tank is untrapped and causes a nuisance injurious to health by the stench which arises through the grate, and also from the WC adjoining the same yard. The dairy window and kitchen door are about eleven feet from the former . . . The first tank is outside and . . . drains into a larger tank or cesspool without any outlet whatever, except for the top which is covered with flags and a thin portion of earth, standing 4' 6" deep in stinking fermenting water.

The authority recommended various improvements which were carried out and, no doubt, a marked improvement was wrought.

Jack Skilbeck was station master at Copgrove from 1907 until 1931. His son Laurie, who was born in the station house a little more than a year after his father became station master, remembers that the staff consisted of the station master, a porter signalman and a lad porter. From 1931 to 1942 Copgrove was managed from Boroughbridge and the staff comprised two porter signalmen only. However, LNER working timetables of the period until the late 1930s contain a note that the daily pickup goods train called at Knaresborough station to take a clerk to Copgrove.

When a station master was restored in 1942 he and the remaining porter signalman covered the work between them, alternating the early and late shifts and with a period in the middle of the day when they were both present. The station master did the station books and undertook the signalling duties when the porter signalman was off duty. The late night Saturdays train kept one man on duty for several hours longer.

Copgrove is remembered particularly for its station gardens. They were, it seems, the creation of Jack Skilbeck. Laurie Skilbeck recalls "the marvellous gardens all down the approach to the station and on the bank opposite the platform" and that his father regularly won a prize in the Best Kept Station competition. This recollection is corroborated by Alec Hardcastle, relief signalman:

Mr Skilbeck was a very, very good gardener and it was a very pretty station. There was a border on the platform, a fairly long one, and Mr Skilbeck filled that with flowers. He had hanging baskets too. The gardens were immaculate, and the offices too. There were prizes for the Best Kept Station and int he North Eastern Area Copgrove always won a Special prize. I can see them even now, the inspectors coming in the 'glass carriage' as we called the inspection

saloon then. Sometimes it was pulled by an engine but they also had a self-propelled one. They would get off at the station and go round it. They would go round everything and see if they could find a little bit of rust here and there. They never did at Copgrove.

Laurie Skilbeck was one child of an extended family of seven children, with more than twenty years between the oldest and the youngest. Not surprisingly most of his memories of Copgrove station are fond ones:

We used to have parties and dances in the ladies' waiting room. It was a big room and of course it had the ladies' toilets in too. After the last train in the afternoon we used to scrub the floor and line it with french chalk so that we could dance on it. We could fit three sets of The Lancers in there. Friends and people from the village came and they would leave their coats in the cloakroom. We used to have to get up early next morning and mop the floor to get the french chalk off again before the first train. (Author's note: in Derrek Trinder's days as station master the same waiting room was used to store the goods and sacks, there being nowhere else suitable.)

I first went to the village school in Staveley but when I was eight years old I went to Priory Street school in York until I was about 16. The most convenient service to York, even from Copgrove, was via Pilmoor. Others got on at Brafferton and Pilmoor, although I don't recall any from Boroughbridge. I left just after seven in the morning and got back at 6.28 at night.

Copgrove's goods traffic was agricultural. A record made in 1913 by the NER shows only that 225 tons of barley were despatched in that year, and no livestock. In 1930 7272 tons of goods were sent out, and a total of 31 sheep in one wagon. If little livestock was despatched, a little more was received. Major L.B. Holliday of Copgrove Hall was a farmer and racehorse trainer. His horses did not come in and out by rail but his cattle are remembered as arriving by rail from Mullingar, in Ireland.

Major Holliday is remembered more for the farm produce that he despatched, including dried grass to Ireland. Dried grass is a pale green colour and oven dried, as opposed to hay which is dried naturally. But hay also went out, arriving from farms in square bales. The farmers paid for the wagon rather than for the weight of what it carried, which was a strong incentive to load as much as possible. For the staff there were conflicting pressures, from the farmers to maximise the load, from the railway company not to exceed the maximum dimensions allowed for a wagon and its load.

Major Holliday was an important customer for railway sacks, whose complications are described in Section 5 of this book. For Derrek Trinder the problem with sacks was getting the farmers to pay.

They'd owe £20 or £30 but it was like getting blood out of a stone. The only way I could get it out of them was when they came for some coal and I'd ask them to add the sack money onto the cheque. But they'd pay me for the coal, but they wouldn't pay the railway for the sacks. So sometimes I had it to pay out of my coal money.

When Derrek Trinder arrived at Copgrove as its new station master he took over the coal sale. As a businessman running the coal sale on his own account, but as an employee making use of the railway's premises, he had to pay rent to the railway. If it was thought that he was earning too much profit the rent would be increased:

In those days my station masters's salary was less than £5 per week; the profit from the coal sale made the difference between existing and living, you might say. I was a coal merchant and there was no competition for coal in the village. I had a dealer who bought it from me in bulk, a welshman, R. Williams. He would buy 15 or even 20 tons a week, about two wagons. He bagged the coal in the yard and sold it to people in the villages round about. I weighed his empty lorry when it came in and the full one when he went out. He came on Monday to pay his weekly bill, and he'd stop and yarn with us. When my porter signalman saw him coming we'd know what to expect! We'd get him a chair and he'd get sat down, and he'd be there all afternoon! As well as the dealer I also sold in bulk direct to some of the farmers and a few individuals. One or two people came with a barrow and I would weigh the odd bag on the scale that was provided.

Potatoes were a staple product of the area and went out in eight-stone bags. In winter the goods staff had to line the wagons with straw, and put another layer over the top, to stop the potatoes from freezing. For a time, round timber — in its natural form when the trees were cut down — was despatched. A timber-loading gang came out from Starbeck to load it. The foreman of the timber gang measured the length and the girth of the timber and estimated the weight from a ready-reckoner book.

Derek Trinder recalls also that "we had empty strawberry baskets. They never sent the strawberries out by rail but they did send the empty baskets back. Sometimes when you took the baskets back you'd be given a big box of strawberries, which were enormous and delicious". For Reg Burton the despatch of swedes and mangelwurzels for making jam was significant: "Today's jam is nothing like it used to be — maybe that's because they don't use swedes and mangelwurzels any more!"

Coal, potatoes, dried grass, timber, strawberry baskets, mangelwurzels, swedes, hay: all to a greater or lesser extent were significant commodities at Copgrove. But the single most important customer may have been Appleyard's Mill, between Staveley and Copgrove villages. The mill processed grain, primarily for animal feed. As the only mill for many miles its catchment was very large. Grain was received direct from the local farms but it also came in by rail to Copgrove station. In the late 1940s large quantities came in under the aegis of the Ministry of Food. For a period, so many wagons of grain did the station receive that the station master had to have them held back at Starbeck until he was able to accommodate them in the yard.

Livestock has been mentioned in the context of the local farms, but there was also the occasional visit from the York and Ainsty Hunt to hunt on the land of Colonel Meysey-Thompson of Spellow Hill. These visits made a strong impression on the then-young Laurie Skilbeck:

When the Hunt came it used to be by train, the horses in horseboxes, and sometimes they brought their food too, with butlers to serve it. The hounds didn't come by rail, because they were in kennels locally. This happened several times a year with a special train each time. Everything, including the horses, was unloaded at the platform. There was a long siding parallel to the main line opposite the platform. When the entire train was unloaded, it was backed into that siding until they were ready to go home again, which was not until about 10 at night.

As far as the passenger business was concerned Copgrove was the quietest of the three stations. But in its early years, as Appendix A shows, the numbers of passengers using Copgrove were as plentiful as those at Brafferton, 32 per day at the peak. In 1940, with only four per day, there was only one possible consequence. There were no regular school children to Knaresborough and only a few work people to Knaresborough or Harrogate. On a Saturday some would use the morning train to Knaresborough or Harrogate and return by the midday Saturday-only train. Others would return by the late night Saturday-only train.

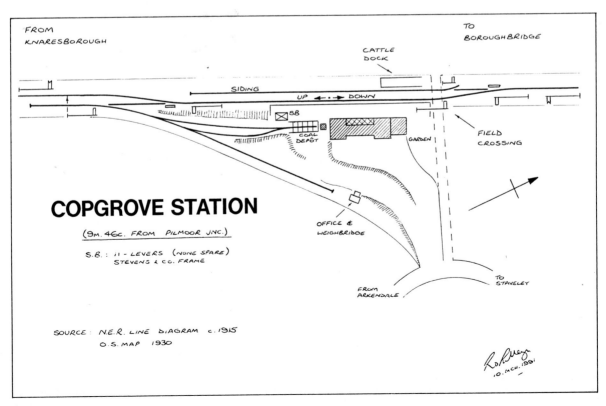

FROM KNARESBOROUGH

TO BOROUGHBRIDGE

CATTLE DOCK

SIDING

UP ← → DOWN

SB

COAL DEPOT

GARDEN

FIELD CROSSING

OFFICE & WEIGHBRIDGE

FROM ARKENDALE

TO STAVELEY

COPGROVE STATION

(9M. 46C. FROM PILMOOR JNC.)

S.B.: 11 - LEVERS (NONE SPARE)
STEVENS & CO. FRAME

SOURCE: N.E.R. LINE DIAGRAM c.1915
O.S. MAP 1930

The Brafferton-bound pickup arriving at Copgrove on May 17th, 1958, then shunting a horsebox into the yard.

(Jim Sedgwick)

Copgrove station was closed to passengers in 1950 along with Brafferton and Boroughbridge. Like the other two it remained open for goods traffic until 1964 but, unlike the others, it was made a 'public delivery siding' in May 1951. For its last thirteen years the station had no staff. The pickup put wagons into the yard and removed them again later, with all the necessary commercial arrangements being carried out through Boroughbridge station. Possibly the most dramatic event in the station's history occurred during its last months, when the pickup was derailed near the station and several wagons of coal turned over and disgorged their loads. The coal that could not be recovered was later sold to the farmer onto whose land it had descended.

Bill Hall and Percy Norton working on the track close to Copgrove station c1946.
(courtesy of Clarrie Fawcett)

Bridge 23, carrying the Ferrensby to Farnham road over the branch, with Bridge 22 in the background, both clearly built for a double line.
(MR 365606)
(John Mallon)

8 Knaresborough Goods Junction

The original purpose of the junction signal box, as its name suggests, was to serve Knaresborough goods station, opened in 1851. When the Boroughbridge to Knaresborough extension was opened on April 1st 1875 it was connected to the York to Harrogate line by a double track junction, in accordance with NER practice. The single line branch became double for a little more than 300 yards, so that the actual junction was between two double lines. Consequently there was a second signalbox at the transition from single to double track, known as Knaresborough North Junction but later renamed Knaresborough Inner Junction.

In 1896 the Inner Junction signalbox was closed and the transition from single to double on the branch was brought close enough for it to be controlled from Knaresborough Goods Junction box. The redundant part of the double line up to the junction was converted into a long siding.

Over the years this siding proved its worth. A complete goods train might be put in, to let a passenger train go by on the main York to Harrogate line. Likewise, goods wagons could be put down there while shunting was going on in Knaresborough's constricted goods yard. During the Second World War a set of passenger coaches for working an early morning Knaresborough to Bradford train was left there overnight. There was a standing instruction that whenever vehicles were put down the siding for a lengthy period a gap should be made where a footpath crossed the line.

In 1916 the local firm of A.H. and E.W. Batchelor, horticulturalist and market garden (no connection with the national company known for its peas), made an agreement with the NER, under whose terms the siding was extended by forty feet and two coal shutes were installed alongside the extension. The coal was used for heating Batchelor's nearby greenhouses. The siding was thereafter known as Batchelor's Siding.

On the withdrawal of the branch passenger service in 1950 Knaresborough Goods Junction signalbox was downgraded. The only regular train on the branch was the daily pickup goods, with an occasional additional goods train but no passenger trains. The two full-time signalmen were replaced by porter signalmen who spent most of their time at the passenger station. When access to the goods yard or the branch was required, they went to the junction and worked the signalbox.

Batchelor's Siding became disused during the 1950s and by 1960 the coal shutes were derelict. But at this time the branch itself had a use other than for the pickup. On Bank Holiday Mondays there were many extra passenger trains to Knaresborough, some of which terminated there. The line to York was so busy that it was expedient to put these empty trains a short distance down the branch, merely to get them out of the way. When there was a lull, or when the empty trains were needed once more, they were brought out again and run back into Knaresborough station. The advent of diesel multiple units in the mid-1950s simplified this operation. The single line Staff was used, even though the trains went only a short distance down the branch.

The branch was closed completely in October 1964. Three months later the siding agreement with Batchelor's was terminated, although the coal shutes had not been used for many years prior to that. Knaresborough Goods Junction signalbox was closed on October 17th 1965.

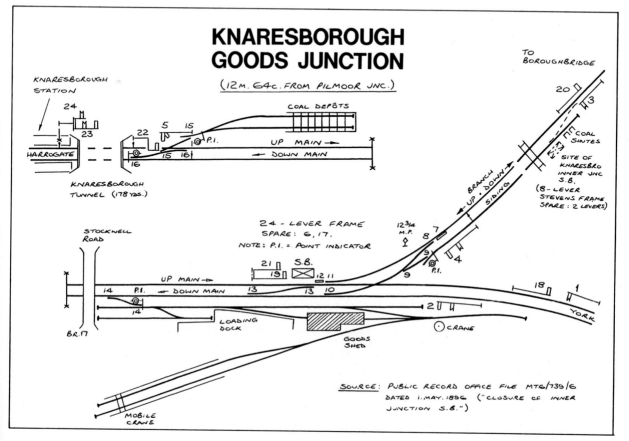

KNARESBOROUGH GOODS JUNCTION

(12M. 64C. FROM PILMOOR JNC.)

SOURCE: PUBLIC RECORD OFFICE FILE MT6/739/6 DATED 1.MAY.1896 ("CLOSURE OF INNER JUNCTION S.B.")

Knaresborough Goods Junction from the end of the branch. The Harrogate to York line goes off to the left; the Knaresborough goods yard with its warehouse is in the background. (MR 354575). *(John Talbot)*

Class B1 locomotive 61049 with a short goods train, passing Knaresborough Goods Junction signalbox. From the attitude of the fireman, possibly picking up the staff, the train may be bound for the branch. *(John Talbot)*

Class G5 0-4-4T No. 67337
coming off the branch at
Knaresborough Goods Junction
with a Pilmoor to Harrogate
train on April 30th 1949.
*(© John Armstrong/courtesy of
the John Armstrong trustees)*

Knaresborough Goods Junction
signalbox.   *(Frank Dean)*

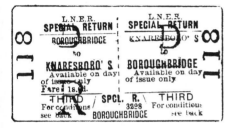

A ticket to Boroughbridge
issued at Knaresborough South
booking office. The North
booking office on the other
platform would have used the
suffix (N).
(Geoffrey Lewthwaite collection)

9 The Goods Delivery Service

From the earliest years the collection and delivery of goods was an important railway activity. In the cities and the larger towns the railway companies maintained a fleet of horse-drawn vehicles for the purpose. In the country the locals generally made their own arrangements. In December 1878, for example, the NER received a memorial from the Market Committee and inhabitants of Boroughbridge asking for free goods delivery in the town. There is no evidence whether this request was met – probably not.

In March 1906 the NER made an agreement with the local Boroughbridge carter James Sadler for the collection and delivery of goods in the town. The contract stipulated that Mr Sadler was to collect and deliver in the central part of the town, radiating from the goods station itself. Within the town no charge was made to the customer but outside Mr Sadler could charge what he liked and keep the moneys earned. The agreement with the NER included a clause to the effect that "the Carter shall at the Carter's own cost provide a horse harness workman and such ordinary things as the Company may consider necessary . . . but the Company shall provide the Carter with and keep in repair a rulley with a rulley cover slides lamp and rope therefor . . ."

On Mr Sadler's death in June 1914 the agreement passed to his son Luke. On Luke's death in April 1931 it passed to his brother Stewart Sadler. The agreement was, however, terminated in February 1933 when the LNER acquired Boroughbridge's first motor lorry. Bob Pinkney came from Pontefract to be its driver. However Sadlers continued to deliver goods around the town with a horse and rulley.

The country motor driver had a close relationship with his customers, most of whom were farmers. On occasion he would receive a small gift of agricultural produce; a dozen eggs was typical. But being a goods motor driver in a country area was no sinecure. The working day was long. The drivers usually had to load and unload their lorries single-handed, and carry very heavy weights, not usually for great distances but often up and down ladders. The work had to continue in all weathers. Joyce Coates (née Pinkney) recalls her father "coming in at eight or nine o'clock at night absolutely soaked through from being stuck in the snow. My mother spent many an anxious time not knowing when he'd be home."

Between 1933 and 1935 Boroughbridge acquired three drivers: Bob Pinkney, Walter Kay and Eric Jackson. The last-named came in 1935 and remained based at Boroughbridge for thirteen years:

There were the three of us but if we were extra busy a driver would come out from Ripon with a big articulated lorry, especially when we were busy with the auction mart. We had rigid and articulated motors. At night we kept them in the goods warehouse and the last man in locked the place up. There was certainly enough work for the three of us, especially as Brafferton came under us. When the traffic at Brafferton grew to be too much for the three Boroughbridge motors they appointed a driver there. This was before the War.

The town was delivered in the mornings, as were the loads that all went to one place. Walter Kay was mostly on through loads with a six-ton articulated motor. Bob and I shared the country service and we took it in turns to do our different runs in the afternoons. Bob did Monday, Wednesday and Friday afternoons. I did Tuesday and Thursday afternoons and Saturday mornings. He started

out from here and did Minskip, Aldborough, Staveley and towards Knaresborough as far as Hay-a-Park, on to Copgrove to pick up at the station there and do all that district. He came back via Great Ouseburn, Grassgills estate, Lower Dunsforth, Upper Dunsforth, Aldborough and into Boroughbridge.

On my run I went to Langthorpe, Kirby Hill, Skelton-on-Ure, Givendale, Marton-le-Moor, Dishforth, Dishforth aerodrome, Norton-le-Clay, Helperby, Brafferton, Cundall, Fawdington, part of Flawith, Myton. Then I came back by Humberton, Milby to Boroughbridge. It was when I got to Brafferton that I picked up the load there for Myton, Cundall and that area.

Every Monday we used to do the auction mart. We used open trucks but we used to put side boards up, a sheet over the top and doors at the end. Arthur Clayton, the chief clerk, used to give us our orders and we collected the sheep, pigs and cattle. Mr Clayton and George Hutchinson, who was a platelayer, used to be in the auction mart when we arrived. George would help in the unloading when we arrived there. We would be told to drop the animals off and he penned them so that we could get away for another load.

At dinnertime on the Monday we washed the motors out. In the afternoon most of the animals went away by rail but we took some to local places. Mr Clayton used to stand in the auction mart to give us our orders and George Hutchinson used to help load them. We took them to the slaughter houses: pigs to Addinghams of Hampsthwaite, cattle and bullocks to Starbeck. There was another at West Park in Harrogate.

When one of the regulars was ill or on holiday we had a relief driver out from York or Harrogate. Mr Clayton would put him on to easy runs, perhaps through loads of grain or potatoes, because he usually hadn't a clue where people lived in the villages. He would direct him on a piece of paper, or ask us to.

We took railway sacks out to the farms. When they were full we mostly fetched them in, after the farmer notified the station that they were ready. It was 16 stone of wheat and barley and 12 stone of oats in a sack. When we took seed wheat to the Franks's farm, in 16-stone bags, we had to climb 22 steps up with the sack and 22 steps down for the next. I wasn't very big but I still had to do it, the same as the others.

Eric Swinn was the motor driver at Brafferton and remained so until the station was closed to passengers in 1950. He was based at York Goods depot and until the start of the Second World War he drove out with a load from York each morning. With the onset of war there was a need to save petrol, so the lorry was kept overnight in one of the coal cells at Brafferton and he travelled out by passenger train. He would usually return to York on the local bus, as the last afternoon passenger train was too early. Being the only driver at Brafferton he delivered everything that went through the station, including passenger parcels. When he was very busy a Boroughbridge-based driver would help out. George Berriman, porter signalman at Brafferton recalls that "every Monday he brought in 30 tons of potatoes from Arthur Mason's farm at Myton. They were in sacks. I remember him saying 'You're humping potatoes all day at work, and then there's a plate of potatoes waiting for you when you get home at night!'"

As well as the motor drivers at Boroughbridge the station goods clerks also had a part to play. Dick Watson was one of them in the late 1950s:

We had a petrol tank outside the office for our motor delivery vehicle. When we had a delivery of petrol we had to put some green dye in it to stop it from being used other than by the railway vehicles. One of my responsibilities was weekly to dip the tank to make sure that everything balanced out. Another responsibility was to record and analyse the driver's log sheets so that at the end of each week we could see how many tons had been collected and delivered, how many miles per gallon of petrol, how many tons per vehicle working day. It was a way of measuring how effectively we were using the vehicle.

As the goods traffic declined so too did need for the delivery service. Bob Pinkney was eventually the last — he had been the first too — when the branch closed in 1964.

Best length certificate awarded to Joe Tuley, ganger in charge of the Boroughbridge length in 1938. *(courtesy of Roy Tuley)*

Brafferton station c1947, with the motor delivery lorry. From the left, Charlie Buck (porter), Bob Gibbons (clerk), Stan Young, Ned Richmond (platelayers), Eric Swinn (motor driver), Arthur "Miff" Leonard (ganger)

10 Trains and Locomotives

Passenger Trains 1847 – 1875

Between 1847 and 1875 the passenger service consisted of a shuttle between Boroughbridge and Pilmoor, where it connected with the main line. (There is some doubt about whether Pilmoor was the destination for the first year or so, as the station is not shown in the 1847 Bradshaw timetable.) The service was based on Boroughbridge whence the first train started out in the morning and where the last train finished at night. There was a locomotive shed there and, for at least some early years, a turntable.

The table below illustrates the changes in the number of daily trains in each direction between Boroughbridge and Pilmoor:

	1847	1850	1855	1858	1860	1861	1867	1870	1872	1874
Weekdays	8	5	3	3	4	6	9	8	7	8
Sundays	2/3*	3	2	0	0	0	0	0	0	0

* 2 in one direction, 3 in the other

The inhabitants of Boroughbridge and its neighbourhood petitioned the NER when, in December 1855, the service was reduced. The petition was unsuccessful; indeed in 1858 the service was reduced further with the final (and permanent) discontinuation of the Sunday service.

In 1867 and until 1875 the late afternoon train ran through to Thirsk and back. When this ceased in 1875 the regular branch service never again ran onto the main line at Pilmoor.

The example below is for the year 1867, when the service was increased to its greatest frequency. The four trains of the 1860 timetable are shown with a *:

		*				*	*		*	
Boroughbridge	dep	0620	0725	0810	1000	1205	1355	1615	1835	1940
Pilmoor	arr	0640	0745	0827	1020	1225	1415	1633+	1855	2000
Pilmoor	dep	0650	0750	0835	1030	1227	1427	1720+	1907	2012
Boroughbridge	arr	0710	0810	0855	1050	1257	1447	1740	1927	2032

+ through to/from Thirsk

1875 – 1950

When the Boroughbridge to Knaresborough extension was opened in 1875 the service covered the whole branch between Pilmoor and Knaresborough but invariably also ran on to Starbeck and Harrogate. Each morning a train started out from Boroughbridge, ran to Pilmoor and then shuttled to and fro between there and Harrogate, before finishing in Boroughbridge at night. In the first few years another train emanated from Harrogate each morning and passed the first train at Boroughbridge, making use of the short-lived passing loop there. This was one of the very few instances of there being two passenger trains on the branch simultaneously. They were never to recur.

In 1886 the orientation changed completely and all trains subsequently were based on Harrogate. The engine shed at Boroughbridge was made redundant and in 1896 it was converted into a goods warehouse.

There were many changes in the passenger service during the 75 years from 1875. The table that follows covers a sample of years. It shows through trains between Harrogate and Pilmoor in both directions. Trains that operated only on certain days or only over a part of the route, or both, are shown by an appropriate footnote. The timebands are defined loosely, with overlaps:

morning	early	up to 0930	afternoon	early	1200 – 1500	evening	early	1700 – 1900
	mid	0900 – 1130		mid	1430 – 1630		mid	1830 – 2100
	late	1100 – 1245		late	1600 – 1830		late	2030 on

H'gate to Pilmoor	morning			afternoon			evening		
	early	mid	late	early	mid	late	early	mid	late
1875	2 a		1	1		1		1	
1883	1 a	1	1			1		1	
1886	1	1	1			1		1	
1895	1	1	1		1 b	1		1	
1904	1	1	1		1 c	1		1	
1913	1	1	1		1 d	1		1	
1918	1		1			1			
1920	1	1 d	1			1		1 e	
1930	1		1 e			1		1 e	
1939	1		1 e			1		1 e	
1943	2 f		1 e			1		1 e	1 g
1950	1		1 e			1		1 e	1 e

Pilmoor to H'gate	morning			afternoon			evening		
	early	mid	late	early	mid	late	early	mid	late
1875	2			1		1		1	1 h
1883	1	1				1		1	1 h
1886	1	1				1		1	1
1895	1	1		1	1 i			1	1
1904	1	1		1	1 j			1	1
1913	1	1		1	1 k			1	1
1918	1					1		1	
1920	1					1		1	1 e
1930	1				1 e			1	1 e
1939	1	1 i			1 e			1	1 e
1943	1	1 l			1 e			1	1 e
1950	1				1 e			1	1 e

a includes one from Boroughbridge only to Pilmoor
b Wednesdays and alternate Tuesdays, from Harrogate to Boroughbridge
c Harrogate to Boroughbridge only
d alternate Mondays, from Harrogate to Boroughbridge only
e Saturdays only
f includes one on Tuesdays, from Harrogate to Brafferton
g Saturdays only, not advertised beyond Knaresborough. For personnel of Dishforth airfield (Boroughbridge) and Brafferton bomb dump
h Pilmoor to Boroughbridge only
i Wednesdays and alternate Tuesdays, from Boroughbridge to Harrogate
j Boroughbridge to Harrogate only
k alternate Mondays, from Boroughbridge to Harrogate only
l Tuesdays, from Brafferton to Harrogate

The above table illustrates how the one constant in the service was a train from Harrogate to Pilmoor and back in the morning and the late afternoon or early evening. The table below shows how the times of these trains changed over the 75-year period:

Year	H'gate dep	Pilmoor arr	Pilmoor dep	H'gate arr	H'gate dep	Pilmoor arr	Pilmoor dep	H'gate arr
1875	0720	0818	0825	0910	1625	1713	1725	1815
1886	0723	0804	0815	0900	1635	1716	1740	1835
1896	0707	0748	0812	0857	1645	1726	1745	1830
1904	0705	0746	0812	0857	1643	1724	1755	1844
1915	0707	0744	0812	0857	1645	1724	1750	1837
1924	0650	0729	0805	0854	1640	1719	1800	1850
1935	0650	0726	0808	0850	1640	1716	1752	1832
1943	0635	0711	0808	0850	1653	1711	1830	1921
1950	0640	0718	0806	0850	1700	1740	1816	1900

For all the years of the passenger service connections were maintained at Pilmoor for York, Darlington and, from when the appropriate branches were opened, towards Malton or Pickering via Gilling. The illustration below is for 1904:

dep B'bridge	arr P'moor	dep P'moor	arr Dar'ton	dep P'moor	arr York	dep P'moor	arr Malton	arr Pickering
0732	0746	0805	0854	0751	0833	0812	0917	1010A
0942	0956			1018	1056	1018	1156B	1202C
1210	1223	1233	1357			1325SO	1430SO	
1710	1724	1735	1847	1743	1810	1748	1902A	1903
2010	2023	2040	2148	2106	2130			

A change at Gilling

B change at Raskelf

C change at Raskelf and Gilling

SO Saturdays only

In January 1939 a paper was considered by the Traffic Committee of the LNER:

The passenger trains on the Harrogate to Pateley Bridge and Harrogate to Pilmoor branches and some of the trains on the Harrogate to Bradford service do not convey a sufficient number of passengers to warrant normal train sets being employed but Sentinel coaches would be inadequate.

It is proposed therefore to introduce two 'push and pull' units, each consisting of an engine and two coaches, with a spare coach. These units are less expensive than ordinary trains because a guard is not required and more journeys can be made during the shift of a driver and fireman, on account of the reduction in terminal time and the general flexibility of the units. The cost of altering two engines and five coaches from our existing stock and equipping them with the necessary controls is £484.

A saving in wages costs at the rate of £768 per annum will be effected and since one coach is rendered unnecessary there will be a further annual saving of £312 in maintenance, renewal and interest charges, making a total of £1,080.

Recommended that expenditure of £484 (Chief Mechanical Engineer) is authorised.

At its meeting of January 5th 1939 the Traffic Committee agreed with the recommendation and push-pull working was introduced in February or March. For the Borough-bridge branch service class G5 locomotive 387 and two coaches were used. The engine was semi-permanently attached to its train and adaptations were made so that the train could be driven from either end. The locomotive and crews were based at Starbeck locomotive depot, with the coaches at Harrogate.

The first morning train ran from Harrogate to Pilmoor and back, but the same train and its crew then continued on to Bradford via Otley, finishing in Harrogate in mid-afternoon. The afternoon train from Harrogate to Pilmoor and back was operated by a Pateley Bridge-based push-pull train and crew. Its schedule was Pateley Bridge – Harrogate – Knaresborough – Harrogate – Pilmoor – Harrogate – Pateley Bridge. Later the afternoon run became a mirror of the morning to Pilmoor and Bradford, with a Starbeck train and crew. Although these arrangements created through services between Pilmoor and Bradford or Pateley Bridge they were not advertised as such.

During busy periods the two-coach push-pull train was replaced by a larger locomotive with four coaches. The extra passenger capacity was required for the Harrogate to Bradford leg of the train's run and four coaches was far more than was needed between Pilmoor and Harrogate. Push-pull working continued until the withdrawal of the passenger service in 1950, but it was not an invariable practice.

Immediately on the outbreak of War in September 1939 the passenger service was severely reduced, in common with services elsewhere. However in December, during the 'phoney war', it was increased again until on Monday 26th February 1940 it was again reduced, even further than in the previous September. The movement of increasing quantities of freight had to take precedence.

Class G5 locomotive 67278 on the 1825 Pilmoor to Harrogate passenger train near Milby August 14th 1947.

(J.W. Hague, courtesy of David Beeken)

Passenger Locomotives

The locomotives that operated the passenger services in the very early years are unknown to the author. In an article in a 1950 SLS Journal B. Richardson recalled that in "the early nineteen-hundreds the Pilmoor-Harrogate trains were entrusted to Fletcher 0-4-4 well-tanks and Worsdell side-tanks of the same wheel arrangement (Class O). A particular old friend was no. 1346, a Fletcher well-tank which worked on this line for many years".

It seems that the Fletcher BTP and Worsdell Class O 0-4-4T (later LNER G5) were the staple locomotive for most of the life of the passenger service. Certainly the G5 was predominant from the late 1930s until the end of the passenger service in 1950. The following individual passenger locomotives of this and other classes are known to have been in use (LNER numbers are given with BR numbers in brackets where relevant):

NER class O, LNER class G5 0-4-4T
    149 (67338), 387 (67340), 408 (67342), 468 (67332), 580 (67334), 1737 (67273), 1881 (67278), 1911 (67289), 1912 (67290), 1915 (67293), 2092 (67321), 1695 (67337).

NER class R, LNER class D20 4-4-0
    712 (62375), 1235 (62392), 1258 later 62394

NER class B, LNER class N8 0-6-2
    267 (69395), 348 (69384)

The Second World War Tuesdays-only train from Harrogate to Brafferton was a Sentinel steam rail car.

Class G5 locomotive 67289 at Pilmoor May 27th 1950.

(J. W. Hague, courtesy of David Beeken)

Goods Trains

The working timetables of the period show no goods trains between Pilmoor and Boroughbridge between 1847 and 1875, although they do for other lines. It is difficult to believe that there were none but presumably any trains that were necessary were put on as specials.

When the Boroughbridge to Knaresborough extension was opened in 1875 there were two daily goods trains, both entering the branch at Pilmoor. The first train left Pilmoor at 0905, arrived at Boroughbridge at 0935 and returned to Pilmoor at 1000. The other train departed Pilmoor at 1255 and ran through to Knaresborough, arriving there at 1410. It left Knaresborough again at 1505 and reached Pilmoor at 1600.

In 1876 the working changed, with one goods train from Starbeck and another from Pilmoor, both trains terminating at Boroughbridge, albeit at different times of day. 1876 also saw the introduction of the first cattle trains from Pilmoor to Boroughbridge and back late in the afternoon.

In 1886 the train from Pilmoor started out from York and served the intermediate stations on the main line between York and Pilmoor before running to Boroughbridge. Before returning to York the train also went to Thirsk. There were two cattle trains when required:

| | Train 1 | | | Train 2 | |
	arr	dep		arr	dep
York	–	0700			
Pilmoor	0830	0845	Starbeck	–	1240
Boroughbridge	0925	1005	Boroughbridge	1330	1445
Roecliffe	1010	1020	Starbeck	1525	–
Boroughbridge	1025	1100			
Pilmoor	1125	1130			
Thirsk	1210	1335			
York	1505	–			

| | Train 3 | | Train 4 | |
	arr	dep	arr	dep
Pilmoor	–	1720		
Boroughbridge	1735	1800	–	2100
Pilmoor	1815	–	2120	2130
Boroughbridge			2150	–

Train 1 served Brafferton, but to Roecliffe on alternate Tuesdays only.

Train 2 served Copgrove and, on the way back to Starbeck, Roecliffe; also to Humberton and Brafferton if required. On alternate Tuesdays departed Boroughbridge 1700, arrived Starbeck 1755.

Trains 3 and 4 were cattle trains, to run when required. Train 3 also started out from and returned to York.

By 1904 all the goods trains emanated from Starbeck. They ran through to Pilmoor and back, serving all the stations and sidings.

Class J39 locomotive 64855 passing under Bridge 23 towards Knaresborough with the return pickup, August 28th 1959.

(Mike Mitchell)

The 'pickup' is a lovingly remembered part of railway lore. Each morning a train started out from some central point that received and despatched long distance goods trains, and progressed along the line, dropping wagons off and picking them up as it went. The Boroughbridge branch pickup remained virtually unchanged from 1904 until 1950. It left Starbeck at about 0900 – the times varied little with the years – and was scheduled to arrive back shortly before or after 1700.

The following example, from 1929, is typical:

	Train 1A		Train 1B	
	arr	dep	arr	dep
Starbeck	–	0900	–	1010
Copgrove	0918	0938	1031	1045
Boroughbridge	0950	1100	1057	1130
Brafferton	1112	1231	1142	1231
Pilmoor	1240	1300	as on	
Brafferton	1308	1315	other	
Boroughbridge	1327	1535	days	
Roecliffe	1540	1550		
Copgrove	1600	1620		
Starbeck	1705	–		

	Train 2	
	arr	dep
Starbeck	–	1355
Boroughbridge	1415	1715
Starbeck	1814	--

Train 1 is the pickup, with 1A its normal schedule and 1B its schedule on alternate Mondays. Both trains served Roecliffe siding when required on the way back from Boroughbridge. Train 2 ran on the same alternate Mondays as 1B. It was a light engine from Starbeck to Boroughbridge, and a cattle train back.

There were several changes between 1935 and 1941. In April 1935 the 0900 pickup from Starbeck commenced running through to Newport, on Tees-side. The return pickup consisted of a 0930 departure from Newport to Starbeck. The trains passed each other at Thirsk or at Otterington and the crews changed over there, but the locomotives worked each train between Starbeck and Newport – out one day, back the next.

In September 1939 the pickup became an out and back working from Starbeck to Thirsk (but also with a through Starbeck to Newport pickup via Ripon, the crews switching over at Thirsk, Otterington or Topcliffe). In 1940 things changed again, with a circular trip in each direction: one train went from Starbeck to Thirsk via Boroughbridge, and back to Starbeck via Ripon; the other did the reverse. The excessive hours put in by the crews with this variant caused the pickup to revert in 1941 to the out and back working from Starbeck to Pilmoor.

Gerry Pierson recalls working the pickup, as a fireman based at Starbeck shed:

It seemed as though, when they laid the railway on that branch, they just followed the lie of the land. Leaving Knaresborough Goods Junction towards Boroughbridge you dropped down and then up through a wild, rocky cutting, completely out of the character with the rest of the country all around. When you were over the top you started to drop down towards the River Tutt. It was quite a steep hill when you were passing Copgrove. If you had 60 wagons you had to put the hand brake on, because if you didn't it was goodbye Copgrove! Coming the other way back to Knaresborough you had to get up that hill through Copgrove but it was very rare that you had to shunt or stop at Copgrove to pick anything up, because you had done it all going.

In 1950, with the complete closure of the line between Brafferton and Pilmoor, the pickup was cut back to Brafferton and as the final years passed it was not unknown for it not to go beyond Boroughbridge.

Goods Locomotives

If the passenger locomotives remained fairly constant, the same cannot be said for the goods. In later years the staple pickup locomotive was the LNER J39 but it was not uncommon for other types to appear. The following individual locomotives are known to have been in use on goods trains on the branch (LNER numbers are given with BR numbers in brackets where relevant):

LNER class J39 0-6-0
   1436 (64860), 1455 (64706), 1460 (64861), 1475 (64855), 1477 (64857), 1480 (64845), 1535 (64935), 1540 (64919), 1551 (64942), 1560 (64944), 1586 (64928)
LNER class K1 2-6-0
   (62056 – not LNER)
NER class R, LNER D20 4-4-0
   1026
NER class C, LNER J21 0-6-0
   973, 1811
NER class P, LNER J24 0-6-0
   1825, 1851, 1957
NER class P1, LNER J25 0-6-0
   1723
NER class P2, LNER J26 0-6-0
   342, 1131
NER class P3, LNER J27 0-6-0
   1044, 1201, 1225, 2347, 2356
NER class Z, LNER C7 4-4-2
   2169
NER class T, LNER Q5 0-8-0
   715, 1218
NER class T2, LNER Q6 0-8-0
   1252, 1257, 1311, 2253, 2280, 2284, 2286
NER class Y, LNER A7 4-6-2T
   1136

Other locomotive types included a former Great Central Railway B7, and an O4. Other types appeared too, sometimes to the considerable surprise of the Starbeck shed crews, among them Tommy Cochrane, fireman:

During the War we used to sign on at about 7.45am for the Boroughbridge branch pickup. But then we'd have to wait for an engine, perhaps for four or five hours after signing on. At that time whatever engine came off the overnight goods from Heaton (Newcastle) you took for the pickup. One morning it was an A4 Pacific. The shed foreman, Jack Cail, said that it was the only engine available and my driver Arthur Lawn said 'I'll take it.' When we got to Brafferton, Lawny said 'I'm not going onto the coal depot with this engine. I could go up onto the depot and before I got the brake on I could be over the far end. I'm not going an inch further than those point ends.' So we came back to Starbeck without shunting the yard at Brafferton. On another occasion we had a 'Green Arrow'.

You left Starbeck every day with up to 60 wagons. With stuff for the stations and the Brafferton dump you used to work 13 hours or more. If we were out for longer than normal we used to be able to get a 'food ticket'; the idea was that you went down into a nearby village and bought yourself something to eat. Sometimes they only reached Brafferton and the drivers used to put in for a food ticket. As soon as you said that you wanted a food ticket the station master at Brafferton told you to loosen off and get back to Starbeck.

Diversions and Special Trains

The Boroughbridge branch was not a regular diversionary route, except in special circumstances. Such diversions as there were usually involved northbound trains only, because at Pilmoor there was no direct southbound running from the main line onto the branch. Even for northbound trains the continued use of Staff and Ticket working was less than ideal. In any case there existed a satisfactory route via Ripon.

On one occasion, well remembered by the staff, among them Gerry Pierson, the LNER W1 'Hush-hush' locomotive 10000, worked out of Neville Hill (Leeds):

In May 1935, over a period spanning the Whit bank holiday the famous Hush-hush was having what was to be a final fling from Neville Hill depot. It was to be seen almost daily in charge of the 0900 Liverpool – Newcastle train, due through Harrogate at lunchtime. During the same period a bridge at South Stainley, on the Ripon line, was being renewed. The new structure was rolled into place at a weekend but the work was incomplete on the Monday morning. Trains were diverted via Knaresborough and Pilmoor, including the Liverpool – Newcastle train in the charge of the Hush-hush, probably the only time that it went over the branch. I would imagine that Sunday trains were also diverted over the branch too that weekend.

There were other diversions but relatively few. More frequent were the special trains. The Barnaby Fair at Boroughbridge, held in June, was one of the early highlights. In 1876, only a year after the Boroughbridge to Knaresborough extension was opened, it lasted from June 13th to 23rd. Two daily horse specials were run from York via Pilmoor from June 13th to 17th, and one from Darlington from June 14th to 17th. The return train to York connected there with special trains to Hull, Leeds, Normanton and Scarborough. In the following week passenger specials were put on from Harrogate to Boroughbridge to relieve the normal passenger trains. Likewise cattle specials were also run.

In the pre-Second World War years there were evening excursions and scenic excursions. Evening excursions tended to be on Saturdays during the darker months, for the benefit of the residents of the areas that they traversed. On Saturday February 15th 1936 one such eight-coach train left Starbeck empty at 1615 for Pilmoor. It departed Pilmoor at 1720 and picked up at Brafferton, Boroughbridge, Copgrove, Knaresborough, Starbeck and Harrogate, arriving at Leeds at 1838. It departed Leeds again at 2328 and reached Pilmoor at 0044 on Sunday morning, eventually arriving back empty at Starbeck at 0133.

A six-coach 'Observation Excursion' left Hull at noon on Sunday May 24th 1936 to Harrogate via Selby, Church Fenton and Tadcaster. It remained at Harrogate from 1337 until 1750 and returned to Hull via Boroughbridge, Pilmoor, Gilling, Wharram and Driffield. It arrived back at Hull at 2124. The itinerary of that train was as nothing compared with another in the same summer, a private charter on Sunday July 5th 1936 conveying the Hull Stevedores' Mutual Aid Society. The 10-coach train left Hull at 0944 and travelled by way of Selby and Leeds to Ilkley where it remained from 1137 to 1600. The return was via Otley to Knaresborough, where it remained for nearly three hours until 1935. One might be forgiven for assuming that it then returned to Hull by the most direct route, but not a bit of it; instead it went via Boroughbridge, Pilmoor, Coxwold, Gilling, Helmsley, Pickering, Malton, Wharram, Driffield, arriving Hull at 2307. The travellers were out for 13 hours 23 minutes, of which 6 hours 10 minutes were spent on the move.

Finally, the branch was used as a convenient route to test new locomotives from the Darlington locomotive works, often on a Friday. They travelled via Ripon to Starbeck, where they stood for a short time before returning via Pilmoor. This route avoided the need to turn the locomotives en route. J39s and 'Green Arrows' are remembered particularly.

The last ever passenger train to use the branch was an excursion, on Saturday April 25th 1964. It was also the first passenger train to go down the branch after the withdrawal of the passenger service in 1950. The 'North Yorkshireman Rail Tour' was chartered by the Railway Correspondence and Travel Society and started from Leeds at 0838. It travelled to Boroughbridge and back, arrive 1002, depart 1017 (but not to Brafferton) and later went via Ripon to Northallerton, to Hawes (the last passenger train to traverse the line from Redmire to Hawes), to Darlington and to Middleton-in-Teesdale, before returning to Leeds via York. The train was hauled by, for the branch, a very unusual locomotive type – LMS Class five 44790.

Class G5 locomotive 67337 at Pilmoor c1949.

(W.A. Camwell)

11 Train Control and Signalling

The object of the signalling system on single lines is to prevent more than one train being on the same section of track at the same time. In its simplest form this is achieved by providing a visible authority known as the 'Train Staff' – a short length of wood or brass – without which no train is allowed to enter a section. Although no firm evidence has been found, it seems likely that the line from Pilmoor to Boroughbridge was worked by Train Staff from the time that the original double line was singled, only a few years after opening. The 1867 Working Timetable refers to Staff stations at Pilmoor and Boroughbridge. The evidence suggests too that until at least November 1872 there were no interlocked signals on the branch.

Train Staff working is only appropriate as a method of control where alternate trains run in opposite directions: the first train taking the Staff, the next bringing it back. For where it is desirable also to allow trains to run one behind another in the same direction over a single line, the Staff and Ticket system was devised. Again, only one Staff is provided for each section, but this has a key attached which unlocks a wooden box containing paper or metal Tickets. The first train into the section is shown the Staff, then handed a Ticket as authority to proceed along the single line. The Staff is handed to the last train proceeding through the section. It is known that this method was employed on the Boroughbridge branch by 1898.

The signalmen at opposite ends of a single line worked by Staff and Ticket communicate with each other by means of single stroke bells, as well as Block instruments to provide a visible reminder of the occupation of the line. Trains are then allowed to enter the section with the Staff or a Ticket if the preceding train has been signalled on the Block instrument as having passed through.

The main disadvantage of the Staff and Ticket system is its inflexibility. If a train runs late, or extra trains are operated without prior notice (for example when a neighbouring main line is blocked and its trains diverted), the Staff may be at the wrong end of the section. To cater for such circumstances, complex systems were evolved using a number of Staffs, Tokens or Tablets, electrically interlocked in instruments so that only one can be used at a time. The Boroughbridge branch was unusual in that it retained Staff and Ticket working almost to the end, whereas many single lines were operated by this system during their early lives but were converted to one of the more advanced systems. This reflects the level of service on the branch and suggests that it had little value for diversionary purposes.

On the opening of the extension to Knaresborough in 1875 the Staff stations were Pilmoor West Junction, Boroughbridge Goods Junction, Boroughbridge passenger station and Knaresborough Inner Junction. As mentioned in Section 2, it is assumed that West Junction was another name for Pilmoor Inner Junction, where the branch went from double to single track and where Staff working commenced. West Junction was dropped from the list of Staff stations in 1881 when, presumably, the single line was extended up to the junction with the main line. Roecliffe siding was listed as a Staff station for a time in the 1880s. By the end of 1880 inerlocking was in place between points and signals at Boroughbridge and Copgrove, but not yet at Brafferton.

At Boroughbridge there was a 770 yard section of track between the Goods Junction and the passenger station. In effect this was a passing loop and it was the only place on the branch where two passenger trains could pass. However, by 1881 an instruction had been issued that the Staffs for Pilmoor to Boroughbridge Goods Junction and Borough-

bridge Goods Junction to Boroughbridge passenger station should be fastened together and used as one "except on special occasions". Tacitly this recognised that the passing loop was no longer required for passenger trains, a fact borne out by the timetable. The loop line further from the station building was converted into a siding. Either one passenger train and a goods train, or two goods trains could still pass at Boroughbridge, however, provided that the passenger train remained on the main platform line; the second train was shunted into the siding or onto the Goods branch.

In July 1886 the Staff stations were reduced to Pilmoor Junction, Boroughbridge Goods Junction and Knaresborough Inner Junction. Boroughbridge Goods Junction was closed in June 1892 and the passenger station became the Staff station. Knaresborough Inner Junction was closed in May 1896 when the Staff station became Knaresborough Goods Junction. Consequently, from 1896 until 1936 there were merely two Staff sections: Pilmoor Junction to Boroughbridge passenger station, and Boroughbridge passenger station to Knaresborough Goods Junction.

Although trains could not *pass* in opposite directions at Brafferton or Copgrove (because each station was in the middle of a Staff section), one train could *overtake* another there if one of them, not a passenger train, was shunted off the main line. For this purpose Brafferton and Copgrove became 'Preceding Places'. Although the Staff sections were from Pilmoor to Boroughbridge and from Boroughbridge to Knaresborough, each Staff section contained two Block sections. A goods train might set off from Boroughbridge to Knaresborough, when it was known that a passenger train was due to follow it shortly afterwards. The goods train would take the Ticket and the passenger train would take the Staff. To avoid delaying the passenger train the goods train would be shunted off the main line at Copgrove. When the passenger train arrived at Copgrove with the Staff it would swap it for the Ticket and proceed with the latter to Knaresborough. The goods train would bring the Staff later. By these means the convention of the Ticket being used by the first train and the Staff by the second was maintained.

The Staffs were invariably kept at the south end of the sections to which they applied, this being the end from which very nearly all trains originated. Occasionally a train or an engine came to a section, only to find the Staff at the other end. The routine was either to wait until a train or a locomotive came in the opposite direction with the Staff or to send someone to fetch it by road. Sometimes a taxi was hired or a station employee with a motorcycle would take it.

The older Staffs were generally made of wood, about 15 inches in length, but later ones were often brass and about a foot in length. The identity of the section to which they belonged was stamped on them. A key was hung by a chain onto the handle of the Staff. This released the ground frames at the intermediate sidings at Roecliffe, Humberton and, from 1938, the Brafferton Air Ministry siding.

One end of the Staff was also formed into the shape of a key that was used to open the Ticket box which, for obvious reasons, had to be kept locked. The box was about 12in x 9in and had a slot in the top through which used Tickets were posted. The Tickets were brass plates with one end formed into a key to release the intermediate ground frames. There were four or five Tickets for each section, each one with a number stamped on it, and they had to be used in numerical sequence. It must have been extremely rare for more than one Ticket to have been used.

To prevent the Staffs from being mixed up they were made visibly different from each other. In 1881, for example, the Staffs consisted of:

Pilmoor to Boroughbridge Goods Junction
Staff with one ring round the middle

Boroughbridge Goods Junction to Boroughbridge passenger station
Staff with two rings round the middle

Boroughbridge passenger station to Knaresborough Inner Junction
Staff with three rings round the middle

The Staff and Ticket system was simple and safe, although potentially dangerous mistakes did sometimes happen. One such mistake is recalled by Jack Walker, locoman based at Starbeck, when he was working a passenger train (and after the Staff stations were changed to include Brafferton and Copgrove – see later in the section):

One morning we arrived at Copgrove from Knaresborough and I said 'Where's the Staff?' And the porter signalman said 'Shut up. I slipped up.' When the pickup goods in front of us had gone down the branch he had been given the Staff for the Copgrove to Boroughbridge section whereas, with us coming up behind him, he should have been given the Ticket. When we arrived at Boroughbridge the goods train was in the yard. It was highly illicit!

Knaresborough Goods Junction to Brafferton single line Staff, with the key used to unlock the siding points.
(author)

At 2 pm on Tuesday February 11th 1936 a fundamental change took place. It was revolutionary in its intention although less so in its achievement. The rationale behind it was that, unless a way of reducing the costs of running some little-used country branch lines could be found, they might have to be closed. It was expensive to maintain a full signalling system with signalboxes and signals, locked with the Block system. If a worthwhile saving could be made a branch might have a more secure future.

Up to that time the Boroughbridge branch had maintained the full panoply of signalboxes and semaphore signals, with three stations, four manned and signalled level crossings and two sidings. The proposal developed by the LNER in 1934, after discussions with the Ministry of Transport, involved dispensing with all conventional signalboxes and signals, except those at Pilmoor Junction and Knaresborough Goods Junction.

To replace the abolished signals at each station there were 'Location Markers', 'Section Limit Boards' and 'Station Boards'. The Location Marker was a little more than half a mile from the station and acted as a fixed distant signal. It consisted of a horizontal board 7ft 6in long by 1ft 6in high, painted in black and white diagonal stripes and studded with white reflective lenses in zig-zag formation. The Section Limit Board acted as the station's home signal, also fixed. It was vertical, 6ft 3in high and 1ft 6in wide, and placed 150-200 yards before the station. It was painted in red and white diagonal stripes, with white reflective studs round the border and three clusters of red reflective studs down the centre. There was a Location Marker and Section Limit Board on each side of the three intermediate stations.

The Station Board, of which there was only one at each station, was mounted in a prominent place, normally on the passenger platform some 12ft 6in above rail level. It was four feet square and was rotated on a vertical axis. The two sides of the board were respectively painted red and white all over. In the centre of the white side there was a 1ft 6in square trapdoor which swung upwards and engaged with a catch at the top of the board. When thus opened it revealed a square green panel; at night a long-burning oil lamp was placed behind a green glass in the centre of the green panel. All the Station Boards were operated manually.

The signalboxes having been abolished, a special key was used to unlock the ground frames that controlled the points into the station goods yard. This key also unlocked the trap on the Station Board so that it could be opened to show the green panel, but the key could only be withdrawn from the ground frame when the points leading into the goods yard were fixed for the main line. Thus the Station Board could only display its green panel or light when the points controlling access to the goods yard were closed.

As a train proceeded along the line the crew looked out for the Location Marker and the Section Limit Board. The train could only proceed past the latter and enter the station if the Station Board could be seen to be showing the green panel or, at night, the green light. When green was showing, the line into the station was clear.

Location Marker board on the approaches to Brafferton from Boroughbridge. The River Swale bridge is in the background, showing clearly how the single line is laid to one side of the double track formation. *(BR)*

Section Limit Board at Brafferton, coming from Boroughbridge. *(BR)*

Copgrove Station Board, with the about-to-become-redundant signalbox behind. The catch that secures the central flap in the raised position can be seen on the upper edge.   *(courtesy of Hugh Murray)*

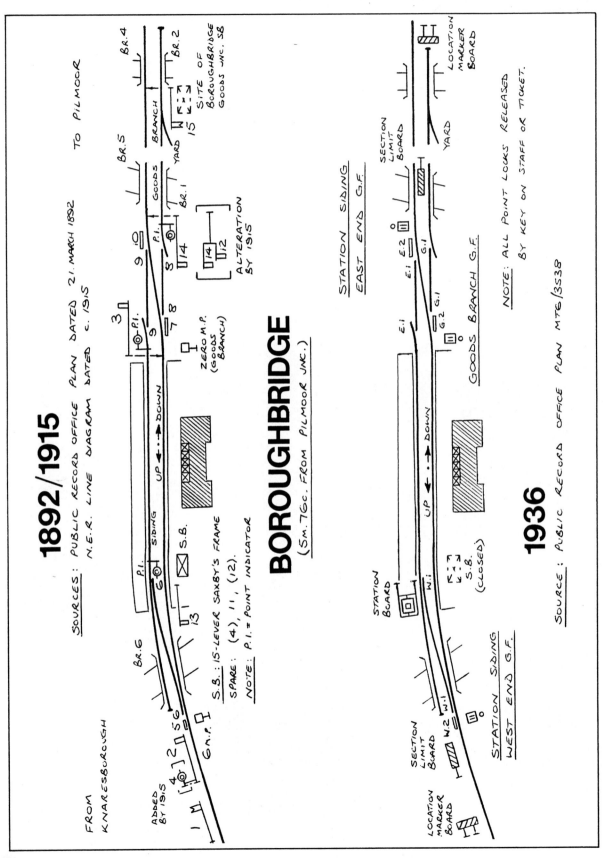

BOROUGHBRIDGE

(5m.76c. FROM PILMOOR JNC.)

1892/1915

SOURCES: PUBLIC RECORD OFFICE PLAN DATED 21. MARCH 1892
N.E.R. LINE DIAGRAM DATED c. 1915.

FROM KNARESBOROUGH

TO PILMOOR

S.B.: 15-LEVER SAXBY'S FRAME
SPARE: (4), 11, (12).
NOTE: P.I. = POINT INDICATOR

SITE OF BOROUGHBRIDGE GOODS JNC. SB

ALTERATION BY 1915

BR.4
BR.2
BR.5
GOODS BRANCH
BR.1
YARD
ZERO M.P. (GOODS BRANCH)
BR.6
SIDING
S.B.
G.F.
ADDED BY 1915

1936

SOURCE: PUBLIC RECORD OFFICE PLAN MT6/3538

STATION SIDING
EAST END G.F.

NOTE: ALL POINT LOCKS RELEASED BY KEY ON STAFF OR TICKET.

LOCATION MARKER BOARD

SECTION LIMIT BOARD

YARD

GOODS BRANCH G.F.

STATION SIDING
WEST END G.F.

STATION BOARD

S.B. (CLOSED)

SECTION LIMIT BOARD

LOCATION MARKER BOARD

Boroughbridge Station Board. The up home signal, about to be displaced by the new boards, can be seen behind. The photographs on pages 56 to 63 were taken before the new Boards were brought into use in February 1936.

(BR)

The four level crossings were marked in a quite different way, each being provided with a 'Gate Caution Board', and a 'Gate Stop Board'.

The Gate Caution Board was about 600 yards from the crossing, one on each side. It was four feet square, painted with two black and two yellow diamonds on a white background. The word GATE was formed by white reflectors across the centre. The Board was pivoted horizontally through its centre. In a vertical position it indicated that the gates were open to the road; in the horizontal position parallel to the ground, and therefore all but invisible to the train crew, it indicated that it was safe to proceed. The Gate Caution Boards, being moveable and some distance down the line from each crossing, were operated by levers in or adjacent to a small cabin at each crossing.

The Gate Stop Boards too were four feet square, painted with a large red diamond on a white background. The word STOP was formed vertically by white reflectors. There was also a red lamp on the gates. At Humberton and Myton Road the crossing gates closed across the railway. The Gate Stop Boards were fixed to the gates; when open to the railway the word STOP was therefore invisible to the train crew. The gates at Pilmoor and Wath Lane did not close across the railway; here the Gate Stop Boards were beside the line adjacent to the crossing and were worked in the same way as the Gate Caution Boards.

To prevent the Gate Caution Board and the Gate Stop Board from being moved to display the 'proceed' aspect when the gates were still open to the road, they were interlocked with the gates themselves. At Pilmoor and Wath Lane a key on each gate had to be removed from the bolt lock when the gates were closed across the road. Only when this was done and both keys had been inserted into the ground frame at the crossing could the Boards be swung to the horizontal position. At Humberton and Myton Road slightly different arrangements applied.

Gate Stop Board affixed to the gate at Humberton crossing, looking towards Wath Lane crossing.   (BR)

The mechanism at Wath Lane crossing for working the combined Gate Stop
Board for Wath Lane and the Gate Caution Board for Humberton.
(courtesy of Hugh Murray)

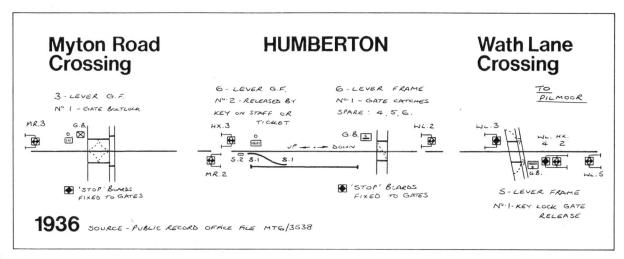

Myton Road Crossing

3 - LEVER G.F.
Nº 1 - GATE BOLTLOCK

'STOP' BOARDS
FIXED TO GATES

1936 SOURCE - PUBLIC RECORD OFFICE FILE MTG/3538

HUMBERTON

6 - LEVER G.F.
Nº 2 - RELEASED BY
KEY ON STAFF OR
TICKET

6 - LEVER FRAME
Nº 1 - GATE CATCHES
SPARE : 4, 5, 6.

UP ← → DOWN

'STOP' BOARDS
FIXED TO GATES

Wath Lane Crossing

TO
PILMOOR

S - LEVER FRAME

Nº 1 - KEY LOCK GATE
RELEASE

The combined Gate Stop Board for Wath Lane and the Gate Caution Board for Humberton, at Wath Lane in the closed (left) and open positions.
(BR and courtesy of Hugh Murray)

Apart from the Station Boards and on the level crossing gates, there were no lights on any of the new signals. Consequently, at night all the trains on the line carried a powerful headlamp, which lit up the reflectors set into the Location Markers and Section Limit Boards at the stations and the Gate Caution and Gate Stop Boards at the level crossings. The Boards at the level crossings were set two degrees off vertical to prevent surface reflection causing interference with the reflectors.

The headlamp was fixed onto the lamp bracket on the locomotive's left buffer beam. Each lamp was nine inches in diameter and equipped with a 6 volt, 24 watt bulb. It was powered by an alkaline battery fixed to the right lamp bracket on the buffer beam. The LNER purchased four lamps, six batteries and six cables from J. Stone and Co. Ltd. of London.

A contemporary comment was that at night the new signals were more easily seen than conventional semaphore signals. But the most startling effect was that of the headlamp shining onto the various markers and boards. The Railway Gazette (February 11 1936) commented that the headlamp "gives a remarkably powerful beam, enabling the boards to be picked up at over 700 yards under favourable conditions".

Simultaneously with the introduction of the new signals, the signalboxes at Brafferton, Boroughbridge and Copgrove were closed. The Block instruments were removed but the bells were retained for communication. Telephones were installed at the level crossings. All the points on the main running lines were worked from ground frames. The line was divided into four Staff sections:

Pilmoor to Brafferton
  Staff with round handle and oval Tickets

Brafferton to Boroughbridge
  Staff with square handle and square Tickets

Boroughbridge to Copgrove
  Staff with round handle and oval Tickets

Copgrove to Knaresborough Goods Junction
  Staff with triangular handle and triangular Tickets

When the Second World War broke out the headlamps were taken out of use. An instruction to the level crossing gate keepers was that, when a train was approaching, they should stand at the crossing and display a red or a white light. The headlamps came back into use after the War.

How, in the memories of the men and women who worked on the line, is this unique signalling system remembered? Harold Hunt, porter signalman at Boroughbridge:

There was many a time when a train was approaching and you were serving a customer with tickets, or dealing with a parcel, and you hadn't time to go out and turn the board. If the signal was against it a train had to stop, but you could guarantee that it would come in, very slowly.

Gerry Pierson, loco man:

The headlamps on the locomotives were really something, although we didn't really bother with them much. They did away with them at the beginning of the War because of the blackout. It didn't really matter as, once we'd got the staff, that was enough as we knew exactly where we were and how far we could go. And even if there wasn't any moonlight you knew where you were.

Dick Potter, relief signalman:

I don't know why they installed the signals, because it didn't save anything. Mr Tattersall was Signal and Telegraph Engineer at the time and I remember that my Dad, who was a signalman at Sessay Wood (near Pilmoor), was visited by him one day. 'What do you think, Fred?' he said. 'Well' he says, 'I'm not being rotten, but all you want is a white horse with a man on it holding a red flag, and we're back where we started!'

An idea of the effectiveness of the powerful headlamp fixed to the buffer beam of a locomotive is shown in this view of the Gate Caution Board approaching Pilmoor crossing from the junction. The Moor siding is on the left.
(courtesy of Hugh Murray)

The special signals and four Staff sections continued in use until the end of the passenger service in September 1950. Shortly after, the signals were abolished, except for the Location Marker Boards and Gate Caution Boards, which remained as permanent fixed distant signals. The level crossings became unmanned shortly afterwards (but Pilmoor crossing was closed completely along with the Pilmoor to Brafferton section).

The remaining line from Knaresborough Goods Junction to Brafferton was initially divided into two Staff sections:

Knaresborough to Copgrove and Copgrove to Brafferton. The latter section was operated under the 'one engine in steam' principle. From September 1951 until complete closure of the rest of the line in October 1964 there was only one section, from Knaresborough to Brafferton, it too worked under 'one engine in steam'. The Knaresborough to Copgrove Staff was subsequently re-used between Barlby North and Cliff Common, on the line from Selby towards Market Weighton, with the original stamped lettering still visible under a coat of paint.

12 The Second World War

Most railway lines were affected in one way or another by the War and special wartime traffic. The Boroughbridge branch's main involvement was in the form of a bomb dump at Brafferton, described in detail below.

When the War broke out the powerful headlamps, used to illuminate the fixed signals on the approaches to the stations and crossings, were abandoned. The train crews were familiar with the route and only at the four level crossings between Boroughbridge and Pilmoor were special arrangements necessary, involving the use of handlamps by the crossing keepers.

At Copgrove Reg Burton did not have any special wartime traffic, but he did see some of the human side of the War:

There was a prisoner of war camp at Riseley, south of Ripon. There were both German and Italian prisoners of war there. A few times when it was very busy, the station master telephoned the camp and asked for some POWs. They came in an Army lorry without a guard. The German POWs were good workers, but the Italians were no good. When we loaded vans of grain in sacks we stacked them two layers high. You had to start the second layer as you did the first, otherwise you couldn't do the second layer. The Italians didn't double them up, but filled the entire floor with one layer.

It was very frightening at times during the War. We often got shot up by German bombers. They used to follow our planes as they returned from raids to Linton, Dishforth and other local airfields. They let fly with their machine guns, presumably because they could see lights. We had a few near misses and I've heard the bullets singing a few times. One night a plane was returning to Dishforth on fire. At the same time there was a German plane coming over, and there was a train coming. With the noise of the engine the train crew didn't know that there was a plane overhead and when I told them after they arrived at the station, they dived out and down between the platform and the train, but the guard stayed in his van.

There were some Irishmen near Staveley, seasonal workers land scratching and potato picking. On Saturday evenings they went drinking in Harrogate and they came back on the late night train, drunk. One night as the train was drawing into the station, I could see one of the doors open before it arrived at the platform and stopped. I saw the flash of the light from inside the compartment. Then one of these Irishmen fell out. 'Mother Jesus, I've gone', I heard him cry out. He fell onto a pile of sleeper chairs at the side of the line and I'm sure that, if he hadn't been drunk and therefore limp, he would have been killed. When he fell out of the lighted coach into the dark outside he thought he'd died!

As early as 1935 construction of the RAF base at Dishforth was commenced. Much of the material came through Boroughbridge station – concrete, bricks and girders for the buildings; hard core and more concrete for the runways. Because of the extra traffic passing through the station extra staff were brought from Starbeck to deal with it. At times eight or nine additional motor vehicles were in use delivering it to the airfield site. Later, during the War, the runways were extended and vast quantities of stone, slack and other materials were brought in.

During the War itself spare aircraft engines and parts for RAF Dishforth came through Boroughbridge station. The base depended on its local railway for many of its basic supplies, coal and food in particular. When a goods train arrived at the station the first question to the crew was "Have you anything for Dishforth?" It might have been in box wagons or in the 'road wagon', the wagon that was a part of every goods train for innumerable years and which carried small items to and from the local stations.

The army too had a presence at Boroughbridge. The Royal Corps of Signals is remembered. Many tanks passed through the goods yard towards the end of the War, possibly because Ripon station was at times too congested and an alternative was required. Trains of up to 30 Sherman tanks were unloaded at the cattle dock at the 1847 passenger station.

Important to the war effort as this traffic undoubtedly was, it pales into insignificance in comparison with the Brafferton bomb dump.

No. 92 Maintenance Unit, R.A.F. Brafferton

This is the full title of the operation known as the 'bomb dump', or 'the Air Ministry siding'. It served as a central supply point for a number of bomber bases in that part of north Yorkshire. In May 1938 the Secretary of State for Air approached the LNER with a view to opening a high explosive storage depot at Brafferton. The full cost was to be borne by the Air Ministry, including for the rail siding.

The land for the dump was requisitioned by the Air Ministry from the Christian Faith Society. The first that the locals heard of it was when a survey was carried out. As luck would have it Maurice Young was involved in the survey:

Just before I started to work as a platelayer on the Brafferton length I went to Leeds for an Army medical. When I was on the way back I met a chap on the train who had surveying equipment. He wanted to know if anyone had a car for hire in the area, and he wanted lodgings for a couple of days. I brought him home and my mother agreed that we could put him up in our spare bedroom in Helperby. I arranged the hire of a car from George Potter, who lived at the top of the village and had this ancient car. He needed it to survey the site of the dump and I went with him. My job was to hold his pole while he marked it out and I had three days wages helping him on that.

RAF Brafferton was part of 42 Group, with RAF Dishforth as its 'parent' station. At the start of the War the dump served RAF Dishforth and RAF Linton; these were joined by RAF Leeming and RAF Topcliffe when they were opened in 1940 and by RAF Tholthorpe in 1943. Supplies were also sent out at various times to RAF stations at Croft, Middleton St George, Thornaby and Marston Moor.

The siding commenced a fraction under two miles from Pilmoor with a connection facing towards Brafferton station. It curved away southwards from the main line and immediately fanned out into three lines. These were the reception sidings and they converged after some 200 yards. The single line continued into the dump and divided into three main sidings, the longest of which terminated near the road from Brafferton to Raskelf. This siding was about a quarter of a mile in length and was straddled by a mobile gantry that was used for unloading the bombs, which were dispersed into underground bomb bays.

The other two sidings were about 150 yards long and ran parallel to each other towards Brafferton Spring Wood. In April 1944 they were both extended by 35 yards. Contemporary plans show that it was intended to considerably expand the dump and its sidings at this time but this was never carried through.

The siding into the dump was officially opened on July 14th 1938, insofar as it was included in the LNER instruction books from that date. However the dump itself was not made operational until August 22nd 1939. Two days later the first three trains of bombs, comprising 64 wagons in all, arrived. On September 1st 42 wagons carrying 250 lb and

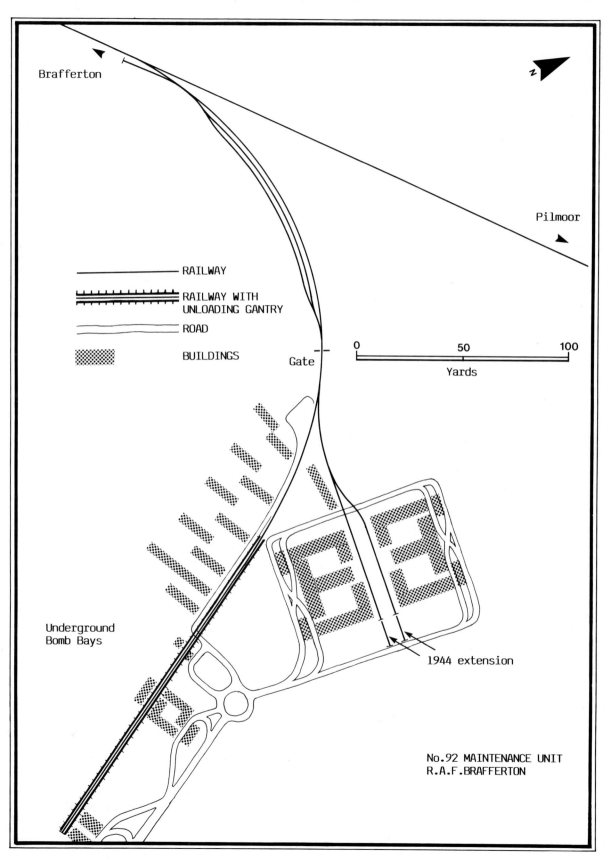

Brafferton

Pilmoor

——————————— RAILWAY

╫╫╫╫╫╫╫╫╫╫ RAILWAY WITH
UNLOADING GANTRY

━━━━━━━━━ ROAD

▒▒▒▒▒ BUILDINGS

Gate

0   50   100

Yards

Underground
Bomb Bays

1944 extension

No.92 MAINTENANCE UNIT
R.A.F.BRAFFERTON

500 lb bombs arrived. On September 2nd work commenced on camouflaging the rail tracks, an act that incensed ganger William Fawcett, who had lavished his skills on laying the sidings, neatly finishing them off and carefully raking the ash ballast, only to find grass seed being liberally spread around. (Problems with camouflage were to haunt the dump: painting the concrete roadways, great areas of netting that were erected and were blown away in a gale.)

As the War progressed it became necessary to find new satellite bomb dumps. In May 1941 a detailed search of the area around both Pilmoor and Brafferton stations was undertaken, with assistance from the station masters concerned. A site at Pilmoor was selected adjacent to the Moor siding, where the first bombs were unloaded in June 1941. It seems that the siding was little used for this purpose and when a larger satellite dump was opened in Sessay Low Wood, behind the railway cottages south of Pilmoor station, the bombs were brought in by road from the main dump.

In August 1942 bombs began to be stored on local roadsides from Brafferton to Pilmoor and also to Raskelf (as well as on countless other country roads elsewhere). Concrete hardstandings were made. Often there was only a small space between separate piles of bombs. Little attempt was made to hide them, although some were covered with a sheet. On one occasion a farmer was fined for burning rubbish between two piles of bombs. As well as the bombs, 'Window', the 10-inch-long aluminium strips that were dropped in quantity from bombers and were intended to confuse the German radar, was also stored in covered heaps. The area was made into a restricted zone, with armed guards and 'ROAD CLOSED' notices at its entrances; the local people were supplied with passes to enable them to pass through. The fact that huge quantities of bombs were stored quite openly along roadsides that were regularly used by the local population caused little consternation, for the bombs themselves were relatively harmless until they were primed.

At the start of the War the amount of bomb traffic into the dump was regular but remained low enough to be mostly conveyed by the normal pickup service. There were occasional full train loads, however, such as on December 28th 1942 when a special train delivered 7900 30lb incendiary bombs and 3500 fuses. But bombs did not only come to the dump by rail; they went out too. For example on February 12th 1943 82 tons were despatched to Glasgow in ten wagons, and 107 tons to Liverpool in nineteen wagons. In general, however, for every two rail wagons received one was despatched.

1943 saw the amount of traffic grow inexorably. The peak was in September and October 1944: between 1st and 11th September 1106 wagons, 13,489 tons, were brought in; the maximum for one day was on October 12th 1944: 99 wagons. The summary below shows how the numbers of wagons in and out grew steadily through the War and declined quickly as it drew to a close. In the years immediately after the end of hostilities wagons were despatched from the dump when bombs, incendiaries particularly, were taken away for dumping at sea.

Summary of Wagons of Bombs In and Out

		In	Daily Ave*	Out	Daily Ave*
1941	Jan – Jun	1218	7	586	3
	Jul – Dec	1527	8	193	1
1942	Jan – Jun	1311	7	575	3
	Jul – Dec	1571	9	784	4
1943	Jan – Jun	2062	11	1118	6
	Jul – Dec	2049	11	1299	7
1944	Jan – Jun	5764	32	2539	14
	Jul – Dec	7648	42	2881	16
1945	Jan – Jun	4799	27	1524	8
	Jul – Dec	147	1	314	2
1946	Jan – Jun	3	0	645	4
	Jul – Dec	41	0	429	2
1947	Jan – Jun	2	0	160	1
	Jul – Dec	5	0	108	1
Total	1941 – 1947	28147		13155	

* assumes 180 days per half year

At an average of eight tons per rail wagon the total tonnage received by rail was circa 250,000 tons.

George Berriman, porter signalman at Brafferton, was actively involved with the extra traffic, both material and human, on the Boroughbridge branch:

At the height of the War in 1944 I seemed to spend most of the time in the dump, shunting. On some days you were in there three times a day. There was a special train in the morning, then the pickup with some more for the dump and another special at four o'clock. Sometimes there might be another at midday. It took up to four hours to deal with a train. The ammunition trains ran on Saturdays, and on Sundays it varied, but on most days there was a special train at four o'clock.

I worked seven days a week and at the end of one week the station master told me that I'd worked 99 hours. To provide relief a man was sent out to take the late shift from four o'clock until it was finished. He was there for a week, learning the job with me. But he complained that, with those bombs and with the wagons being banged about a bit, it wasn't safe. So he went off and wouldn't work the dump. I said 'If one of those bombs goes off you won't know anything about it!' He was frightened, but the bombs weren't detonated and were quite safe. He was there a week and the station master asked me how he was getting on. I said 'He'll never do it. He's frightened. He doesn't want the job.' And so I carried on. The guards didn't like it either or they were useless at it, so it was up to me every time. If you don't want the job, it pays to be useless at it, doesn't it?

When a train for the dump arrived at Brafferton station I rode down with it. We took the train Staff. As you left the main line at the entrance to the dump there were three reception lines. If it was a long train we occupied two of them. When the points were closed behind the train, someone had to walk back to the station with the Staff, because a passenger train might have to go past to Pilmoor. The Staff would have to be brought back later to let the train back out of the dump.

The wagons of bombs were sheeted and, when they arrived in the dump, the sheets were untied only on one side and thrown over the other side of the wagon so that the bombs could be unloaded. We had to fetch the wagons out like that and, when we got them to Brafferton station, we had to take the sheets off properly, in the wind or the rain if it was bad weather. We got the station master to have a word with the Commanding Officer and he arranged to have all the sheets taken off properly, folded up and loaded into an empty wagon, and to write 'sheets' on it. One thing about that was that we were never short of sheets at Brafferton, even though there was a general shortage at other places.

For the locomen the task was similar but with a different emphasis. Jack Walker and Tommy Cochrane:

The gate into the dump was always locked and you had to whistle for the fellow to come and open it. They didn't have their own locos so we had to move the wagons around for them. Before you shunted you had to hand over your cigarettes, matches, lighter. There was a sergeant in charge and it was a Geordie and a Cockney alternating. The sergeant got on to the footplate and he watched every movement you made. You couldn't look out of the cab unless he told you to. One day it was snowing like hell, and there was a lot of snow on the ground. It was the Geordie sergeant and we stood there and we kept hearing this thud, thud, thud. We wondered what was going on, hoping that it wasn't bombs falling out of the wagons. He put his head out of the side of the engine cab and it was the lads dropping coal off the tender. It was so cold for them that they climbed up onto our tender and were chucking all the lumps of coal off and stowing it away in their huts. The sergeant started playing hell and he made them put every bit back!

So much for the work at the dump. For Mrs Eleanor Watson, gatekeeper at Pilmoor level crossing, the dump created a special kind of problem:

The dump was between Brafferton station and my crossing; the bell used to ring in the house when the train was leaving Brafferton station for the dump. But there was no bell to tell me when it was leaving the dump and coming on towards me. Sometimes it was an hour, sometimes three hours. So I had to be on watch all the time for it coming but I had children to look after, and housework too. The train would stop at the crossing because I left the gate open to the road traffic. The crew didn't say anything because they realised that, as there were no more bell signals, I couldn't tell when the train would be leaving the dump.

In April 1942, when the unit strength of the dump was some 280 men, the Commanding Officer approached the LNER with the request for a late train on Saturday nights, so that his men could enjoy the evening delights of Harrogate. This was agreed and the train commenced running in May. It left Harrogate at about 2240 each Saturday night and arrived at Brafferton at 2311.

With the bomb traffic George Berriman, porter signalman, might have had a busy enough time but he had the airmen too:

It wasn't very nice on your own at night with that lot. You didn't know what they were going to do next. One Saturday night a lot of RAF men came off the train drunk and they started fighting. I went in to get the Staff and to pass the train on to Pilmoor and they jammed me into the corner with their fighting. I said 'If you don't let me out of here someone's going to suffer.' And they went out, only to start again in the waiting room. I did all that I had to in the office, and the train left, and I then telephoned the police, but the policeman's wife answered. 'I'm sorry' she said 'he's out at a fight somewhere else.' With that Mr Pratt, the station master, came in, having heard the commotion. There was one of those thick, heavy pint mugs sitting on the end of the desk. He picked it up and threw it at a bloke in the corner. He hit him fair on the head: talk about his knees giving way! He sank down. I said 'you're a bit rough'. He said 'he won't be much more bother'. He got on the 'phone to the CO of the camp and they came down and sorted them out.

When the War ended the dump remained in use for several years although, as the figures above show, the amount of traffic fell off very quickly. In 1950 the section of line between Brafferton and Pilmoor was closed completely but, as the dump was still nominally in use, it was only between there and Pilmoor that the line was taken up. Between Brafferton and the dump the line was treated as a 'shunting ground'.

The dump siding remained officially open until September 13th 1956 but Jack Thompson, who was CO from 1949 until 1952, does not recall any usage whatever during that period. It is unlikely that any part of it was used in its last years, other than a convenient place to store rail wagons.

13 Closure

The introduction of simplified signalling in 1936 was due to the need to reduce costs. There were few trains on the branch – two daily passenger trains in each direction, with two more on Saturdays; one goods train each day and a weekly cattle train.

That there were so few trains is indicative of the level of passenger business. The numbers increased during the Second World War, particularly from Dishforth airfield and the Brafferton bomb dump. But once the War was over decline again set in. In April 1950 the North Eastern Region of BR proposed closure. In the words of the internal memorandum:

Passengers are mainly occasional bookings to Knaresborough and Harrogate, with some inward travel on the late Saturday evening train. Some long-distance travel occurs in the holiday months. RAF warrant and recreational travel is slight . . . There is little chance of increased passenger travel to justify the cost of providing the more frequent service which would be required. Boroughbridge is the only town of any size and its position on the Great North Road makes it an excellent centre for both long and short distance journeys by road. RAF personnel at Brafferton are not numerous and those to and from Dishforth connect with rail normally at Ripon or Thirsk.

The number of journeys from stations on the branch in 1947 and 1948 was approximately 87 per week, or 15 per day. With four trains per day on Mondays to Fridays, with nine on a Saturday – 29 per week – the average per train was a mere three. Incoming journeys added to the numbers but no branch line could survive on fewer than ten passengers per train. Originating passenger revenue was £675 in 1947 and £671 in 1948.

It was estimated that closure would save £6,387 per annum, perhaps as much as £100,000 at 1991 values; the train working costs alone amounted to four times the revenue. It is no wonder that closure appeared to be the only realistic option. But why was the branch so poorly used? There are probably two main reasons. Firstly, between Boroughbridge and Knaresborough there is a road that serves the villages of Minskip and Ferrensby, and is close enough to Staveley, Arkendale and others to be more convenient than the railway. There is a bus service on this road. Secondly, for long distance travel York was the obvious main line railhead. However, travelling to and from York involved changing trains en route, either at Pilmoor or at Knaresborough.

The BR report of April 1950 recommended withdrawal of the passenger service. However there was sufficient goods traffic to warrant keeping the line open, albeit that the two miles between Pilmoor and the Brafferton Air Ministry siding were recommended for complete closure. The passenger service ceased on Saturday September 23rd 1950.

Observations of the amount of passenger traffic during the last weeks confirms the evidence of the figures. Chris Wilson travelled from Harrogate to Pilmoor on Tuesday May 30th 1950, and found "to my dismay the train was packed. However several people got off at Starbeck and Knaresborough. Thereafter traffic was as follows: Copgrove 1 on, 6 off; Boroughbridge 3 on, 2 off (including a woman who had got on at Copgrove); Brafferton 5 off; Pilmoor 2 off." 15 people had used the branch stations. At Pilmoor nine people joined the train for its return to Harrogate.

The Railway Observer of December 1950 recorded that during the last week "journeys were made on the branch by many enthusiasts, particularly on the last day. Of the last trains on 23/9/50 all arrived at Pilmoor with large numbers of passengers, except the 7.45 pm from Harrogate." The locomotive that hauled most of the trains on that last day was G5 0-4-4T 67289 which, as LNER no. 1911, had worked the last passenger train on the Masham branch nearly twenty years earlier. The last train of all, the 2252 from Harrogate to Pilmoor, was worked by G5 67337.

The Knaresborough Post in its issue of 30th September recorded that "the last train to Pilmoor left no. 6 platform at Harrogate. Mr Jack Drury of Knaresborough, who had been on the Pilmoor run regularly for the past 20 years, was the driver. Mr Mark Bradley was fireman. The guard, Mr A. Hare, has travelled on the same line for 31 years. In the two coaches were nearly 150 passengers. The last train to Pilmoor was almost rivalling Blackpool illuminations in its popularity. There was regret in the crowded compartments." The report went on to quote several of the travellers' complaints that high fares and the lack of sufficient trains had driven away the potential business, the conspiracy theory that invariably accompanied branch line closures.

A 'special correspondent', wrote in the *Knaresborough Post* a week after closure:

For many years the line served this land of snug farms and fertile lands – at one time doing a brisk passenger trade, taking the farmers and their wives to the markets, and the young 'uns up to town for a night out! That, however, was before the bus – the executioner of so many railway byways.

I travelled to Pilmoor on the last daylight train from Harrogate to Pilmoor. For the benefit of loco-spotters and rail-fans, 0-4-4T No. 67289 was at the head of three coaches . . . Leaving the main line at Knaresborough, our single line, laid over undulating fields, ran to Boroughbridge, where, before entering the station, our loco gave an impatient steamy sniff at the diesel lorries slowly crawling up and down the A1, Britain's main trunk road.

Calling next at Brafferton, which like Copgrove further down the line was sleeping peacefully in the autumn sun, we galloped onwards towards the distant Cleveland Hills, only to stop short, as with a last defiant shriek of the whistle we rounded the bend leading into Pilmoor, a station on the London-Edinburgh East Coast route.

The line between the Brafferton Air Ministry siding and Pilmoor was removed; at Pilmoor the first 500 yards of the branch was retained as a siding from the East Coast Main Line. The goods service remained, but in a slow decline.

The pickup departed Starbeck at 0915 each day, ran to Brafferton, calling at each station as required. After leaving the branch it went on to Pateley Bridge, before returning to Starbeck some time during the late afternoon. Livestock traffic continued and the Tuesdays-only cattle train left Starbeck at 1150 and returned from Boroughbridge at 1707. In the last years special cattle trains became a thing of the past.

Bit by bit the branch wound down. Copgrove station became unstaffed in 1951. By the late 1950s the pickup had become a three-day-a-week operation, only proceeding beyond Boroughbridge to Brafferton when required. It was not unknown for the locomotive to propel – push – its few wagons to Brafferton. At a time when considerable numbers of goods wagons of all types were being scrapped, a train load of condemned wagons would occasionally be brought down the branch to be stored between Brafferton station and the Air Ministry siding. At Brafferton the locomotive 'roped the wagons by', and then propelled them towards the dump.

Harold Hunt and Charlie Buck, the last men to work the yards at Boroughbridge and Brafferton respectively, found little to do during the last year or so. Charlie Buck worked elsewhere, acting as a relief porter; Harold Hunt sometimes did nothing all day, for there was nothing to do, although he sometimes worked for George Wright, a local coal merchant who used several coal cells at the station.

In 1962 a new bridge was built over the line just south of Boroughbridge, a part of the new A1 bypass round the the town. It was a waste to have to bridge a line whose future was to be so short.

The end came in 1964. On April 25th that year the branch saw its only passenger train since 1950, the 'North York-shireman Rail Tour', chartered by the Railway Correspondence and Travel Society. It went to Boroughbridge and back (but not to Brafferton), then later to Hawes and Middleton-in-Teesdale.

Final closure came on October 5th 1964. The official closure date was a Monday, the first day when trains did not run on the line. The last train was on Friday 2nd October. Thus ended the 117-year history of the railway from Pilmoor to Knaresborough.

The last passenger train to use the branch, an RCTS special "The North Yorkshireman Rail Tour" headed by Class 5 locomotive 44790, in the goods yard at Boroughbridge.
(Jim Sedgwick)

A view of the Boroughbridge goods yard from the last passenger train on April 25th 1964.
(author)

The platform of Boroughbridge passenger station as the last train passes through on its way back to Knaresborough. A short length of bunting decorates the station building but the overall air is one of gloom in the dull weather.

(author)

The last passenger train headed by Class 5 locomotive 44790 leaves Boroughbridge passenger station.

(courtesy of John Bateman)

Appendix A – Traffic Handled at Stations

The figures set out below represent a sample of years, starting in 1885. All are compiled from the records of the NER and LNER, held at the Public Record Office (PRO). The difficulty in compiling such data from a variety of sources is in consistency. The treatment of passenger season tickets is an example. There is no mention of these in the heading "tickets sold" at stations. Yet, from other archive material at the PRO it is certain that these figures do not include seasons. Consequently they have been added, making the assumptions stated. The averages are based on six-days-a-week operation, there being no Sunday service; therefore 313 days per year.

PASSENGER

PILMOOR (A)

year	tickets sold	season (B) tickets	average per day
1885	4,300		14
1890	4,920		16
1895	4,941		16
1905	3,440		11
1910	3,563		11
1915	3,507		11
1920	3,852		12
1925	2,887		9
1930	2,910	810	12
1935	1,638	650	7
1940	1,611	550	7

BRAFFERTON

year	tickets sold	season (B) tickets	average per day
1885	8,669		28
1890	10,420		33
1895	9,066		29
1905	8,398		27
1910	9,097		29
1915	9,042		29
1920	8,087		26
1925	5,505		18
1930	3,976	1,012	16
1935	2,656	1,350	13
1940	3,572	500	13

BOROUGHBRIDGE

year	tickets sold	season (B) tickets	average per day
1885	22,883		73
1890	24,007		77
1895	24,412		78
1905	23,763		76
1910	23,057		74
1915	21,006		67
1920	23,689		76
1925	16,542		53
1930	5,160	3,498	28
1935	2,889	2,688	18
1940	3,803	750	15

COPGROVE

year	tickets sold	season (B) tickets	average per day
1885	8,266		26
1890	10,038		32
1895	9,937		32
1905	9,267		30
1910	8,963		29
1915	8,088		26
1920	8,474		27
1925	5,673		18
1930	2,385	2,565	16
1935	1,444	300	6
1940	1,162	0	4

Notes:

A The numbers at Pilmoor include passengers travelling on Main Line trains.

B There are no records of season tickets in the early years. In 1930, 1935 and 1940 the numbers are based on an assumed number of daily journeys for each duration of ticket; for example 50 journeys, or 25 tickets, for a monthly season ticket. It must be remembered that until the 1960s a six-day working week was normal.

POPULATIONS AND NUMBERS OF PASSENGERS

	population		passengers per year	
	1911	1921	1911	1921
Boroughbridge	3,472	3,398	22,089 6.4(C)	18,101 5.3(C)
Brafferton	1,218	1,130	7,684 6.3(C)	6,415 5.7(C)
Copgrove	463	455	9,568 20.7(C)	7,501 16.5(C)

THE YEARS LEADING UP TO CLOSURE

	1935	1937	1940	1947	1948
passenger journeys		12,145			
passenger tickets sold	6,989		7,537	4,542	4,477
season tickets sold		(D)400		10	11
tickets collected		11,680		8,241	8,197

Notes:

C average number of journeys per head

D actually 4800 season ticket journeys, therefore assumes that the tickets are weekly ones, at 12 journeys per week.

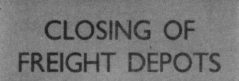

British Railways

NORTH EASTERN REGION

CLOSING OF FREIGHT DEPOTS

The North Eastern Railway Board announce that the following freight depots will be closed on and from Monday, 5th October, 1964, and alternative facilities provided as shown:-

Further information may be obtained from the Divisional Manager, Leeds — telephone 31711

Poster advertising the withdrawal of freight services from Copgrove public delivery siding, Boroughbridge, Humberton public delivery siding and Brafferton from October 5th 1964. *(author)*

GOODS

PILMOOR & BRAFFERTON

year	PILMOOR tons out	tons in	coal/coke(E)	BRAFFERTON tons out	tons in	coal/coke(E)	live/stock(F)
1885	441	266	635	2,431	1,845	1,747	846
1890	774	417	265	2,673	3,482	1,742	4,593
1895	760	364	199	2,352	3,698	1,577	4,261
1905	637	340	(G)	3,077	4,298	(G)	(G)
1910	1,250	700	270	3,667	4,433	2,154	(G)
1915	1,046	348	247	3,351	2,937	2,046	(G)
1920	954	491	148	3,377	2,731	1,673	(G)
1925	514	1,160	210	2,895	5,359	1,673	(G)
1930	1,168	341	139	4,451	1,976	1,805	99
1935	1,002	174	93	4,199	1,548	950	83
1938	219	39	61	1,316	3,819	1,082	65

Pilmoor had no livestock whatever in most years.

BOROUGHBRIDGE & COPGROVE

year	BOROUGHBRIDGE tons out	tons in	coal/coke(E)	live/stock(F)	COPGROVE tons out	tons in	coal/coke(E)	live/stock(F)
1885	10,702	8,436	6,242	19,710	468	1,240	1,700	1
1890	12,814	8,941	7,331	15,730	792	1,185	1,501	3
1895	14,873	10,388	8,346	13,826	687	2,226	1,398	1
1905	14,909	9,302	(G)	(G)	804	1,996	(G)	(G)
1910	18,588	10,502	9,154	(G)	1,221	2,782	1,138	(G)
1915	12,125	9,432	7,438	(G)	968	2,383	1,127	(G)
1920	12,746	17,658	7,248	(G)	890	1,814	1,118	(G)
1925	11,103	25,408	8,746	(G)	1,365	2,479	1,148	(G)
1930	16,509	12,591	4,266	1,233	1,215	2,411	1,039	1
1935	9,399	7,249	3,244	800	897	3,318	378	3
1938	2,565	6,788	3,744	755	405	4,499	250	11

Notes:

E   coal/coke is for tonnage out and in, but, as none of these stations produced coal, it is assumed that it was all received.

F   livestock is measured in wagons, rather than tonnage

G   figures not recorded.

TONNAGES OF GENERAL MERCHANDISE IN 1913, 1923 & 1924

	Brafferton 1913	1923	1924	Boroughbridge 1913	1923	1924	Copgrove 1913	1923	1924
Potatoes	963	2623	1685	1460	4537	2811	(H)	698	472
Barley	485	249	240	1014	839	790	225	146	185
Grain	190	373	294	558	453	390			
Hay, Clover etc.	251	216	289	477	517	640	(H)	242	388
Oats	115	145	188	292	466	532	(H)	171	188
Wheat				216	616	267	(H)	189	(H)
Bulk vegetables	(H)	(H)	168	(H)	148	346	(H)	(H)	128
Seeds			116(J)	96					
Livestock (wgns)	170	53	81	981	1336	1545			
Gravel, sand				(H)	(H)	190			
Sanitary tubes (K)				4079	1761	1972			
Bricks (K)				2847	896	2058			
Ale/ale empties				699	(H)	(H)			

Notes:

H   some traffic, but less than 100 tons

J   February – December 1923

K   presumably from Roecliffe brick and tileworks

LIVESTOCK IN 1930

	Total wagons	calves	cattle	sheep	pigs	horses
Brafferton	99	8	388	1,837		
Boroughbridge	1,233	127	5,421	15,383	391	1
Copgrove	1			31		

Appendix B – Station Masters

(Where a year is shown in brackets it is guessed at with a good degree of certainty. A * after the year indicates that the man is known to have been at the station in the year given. A ? indicates that the date cannot be guessed at.)

PILMOOR

Potts	(1847)	–	1854	R. Dale	1932	–	1933
G. Petch	1854	–	?	F. Gillery	1933	–	1940
J.T. Pratt	?	–	1866	W. Rex	1940	–	1943
C. Edmonds	1866	–	1866	T. Hobkinson	1943	–	?
J.F. Pratt	1866	–	1868	F. Newlove	?	–	1947
J. Sharpe	1868	–	(1875)	W. Lake	1947	–	1950
J. Wilson	1875	–	(1877)	L. Temple	1950	–	1955
J.C. Wilkinson	1877	–	1882	J. Hugill	1955	–	1958
W. Tomlinson	1882	–	?				
R. Richardson	?	–	1889	**BRAFFERTON**			
J.E. Parnaby	1889	–	1892	W. Pullan	?	–	1885
J. Hemingway	1892	–	1898	J. Horsley	1885	–	(1901)
J.W. Cowper	1898	–	1903	N. Raw	1901	–	1929
J.T. Bates	1903	–	1906				
A. Moody	1906	–	1911	Controlled by Boroughbridge 1929-36			
J.G. Parkin	1911	–	1913				
R. Dale	1913	–	1917	J.E. Jackson	1936	–	1938
J.W. Martin	1917	–	1919	R. Pratt	1938	–	1945
C.B. Mowforth	1919	–	1925	W.S. Smith	1945	–	1947
A. Wastell	1925	–	1932	S. Hunsley	1947	–	1955

Joined with Raskelf in 1932

Controlled by Boroughbridge 1955-64

BOROUGHBRIDGE

J. King	1865*	–	1874
J.W. King (son)	1874	–	1885
R. Elliott	(1885)	–	1903
J. Deans	1903	–	1904
T.F. Smith	1904	–	(1912)
M.W. Seymour	1912	–	(1922)
R. Cawood	1922	–	1933
A.F. Johnson	1933	–	(1936)
C.B. Bainbridge	1936	–	(1940)
D.A. Macpherson	1940	–	1954
W.A. Watson	1954	–	1964

COPGROVE

J.T. King	1875	–	1875
G. Mennell	1875	–	1896
T. Bowman	1896	–	1902
J. Ramsay	1902	–	1902
W.R. Brown	1902	–	1907
J.T. Skilbeck	1907	–	1931

Controlled by Boroughbridge 1931-42

W. Greensmith	1942	–	1945
J.E.W. Fatkin	1945	–	1947
M. Braithwaite	1947	–	1948
V.D. Trinder	1948	–	1950

Controlled by Boroughbridge 1950-64

Unstaffed 1951-64